MEMOIRS

OF THE

LIFE

OF THE LATE

GEORGE FREDERIC HANDEL.

To which is added,

A CATALOGUE of his WORKS,

AND

OBSERVATIONS upon them.

Ἐγὼ δ' οἶδα μὲν, ὡς αἱ ὑπερβολαὶ μεγέθυς Φύσει ἥκιστα καθαρχί. Τὸ γὰρ ἐν παντὶ ἀκριβὲς, κίνδυνος ζμικρότητος. LONGINUS.

- - - - - · - - - -
Untwisting all the Chains that tie
The hidden Soul of Harmony.

MILTON.

LONDON:

Printed for R. and J. DODSLEY, in *Pall-Mall.*
M. DCC. LX.

John Mainwaring.

Memoirs of the
Life of the late
George Frederic Handel
First published London, R. and J. Dodsley, 1760.
Republished Travis & Emery 2007.

Published by
Travis & Emery Music Bookshop
17 Cecil Court, London, WC2N 4EZ, United Kingdom.
Tel. 020 7240 2129
From outside UK: (+44) 20 7240 2129
neworders@travis-and-emery.com
Hardback: ISBN10: 1-904331-28-9 ISBN13: 978-1904331-28-5
Paperback: ISBN10: 1-904331-29-7 ISBN13: 978-1904331-29-2

MEMOIRS

OF THE

LIFE

OF THE LATE

George Frederic Handel.

Anno ætat: 56.

MEMOIRS

OF THE

LIFE

OF THE LATE

GEORGE FREDERIC HANDEL.

To which is added,

A CATALOGUE of his WORKS,

AND

OBSERVATIONS upon them.

Ἐγὼ δ᾽ οἶδα μὲν, ὡς αἱ ὑπερβολαὶ μεγέθυς Φύσει ἥκιϛα καθαρκί. Τὸ γὰρ ἐν παντὶ ἀκριβὲς, κίνδυν۞ (μικρότητ۞. LONGINUS.

- - - - - - - -

  Untwisting all the Chains that tie
  The hidden Soul of Harmony.
        MILTON.

LONDON:

Printed for R. and J. DODSLEY, in *Pall-Mall*.
M. DCC. LX.

MEMOIRS

OF THE

LIFE

OF

George Frederic Handel.

GEORGE FREDERIC HANDEL was born at HALL, a city in the circle of Upper-Saxony, the 24th February 1684, by a second wife of his father, who was an eminent surgeon and physician of the same place, and above sixty when his son was born. He had also one daughter by the same wife. HANDEL always retained the strongest affection for this sister, to whose only daughter, *i. e.* his niece now living, he bequeathed the greatest part of his ample fortune.

While he was yet under seven years of age, he went with his father to the Duke of Saxe-Weisenfels. His strong desire to pay a visit to his half-brother, a good deal older than himself, (for we have before observed that he was the issue of a second marriage) and at that time valet de chambre to the Prince, was the occasion of his going. His father intended to have left him behind, and had actually set out without him. He thought one of his age a very improper companion when he was going to
the

the court of a Prince, and to attend the duties of his profeffion. The boy finding all his folicitations ineffectual, had recourfe to the only method which was left for the accomplifhment of his wifh. Having watched the time of his father's fetting out, and concealed his intention from the reft of the family, he followed the chaife on foot. It was probably retarded by the roughnefs of the roads, or fome other accident, for he overtook it before it had advanced to any confiderable diftance from the town. His father, greatly furprifed at his courage, and fomewhat difpleafed with his obftinacy, could hardly refolve what courfe to take. When he was afked, how he could think of the journey, after fuch a plain refufal had been given him; inftead of anfwering the queftion, he renewed

newed his intreaties in the moſt preſſing manner, and pleaded in language too moving to be reſiſted. Being taken into the chaiſe, and carried to court, he diſcovered an unſpeakable ſatisfaction at meeting with his brother above-mentioned, whom till then he had never ſeen.

This was not the firſt inſtance of the father's ill ſucceſs, when he judged it expedient to oppoſe or over-rule his ſon's inclinations. This matter demands a more particular explication, before an account can properly be given of what afterwards paſſed at the court of Weiſenfels.

From his very childhood HANDEL had diſcovered ſuch a ſtrong propenſity to Muſic, that his father, who always intended him for the
ſtudy

study of the Civil Law, had reason to be alarmed. Perceiving that this inclination still increased, he took every method to oppose it. He strictly forbad him to meddle with any musical instrument; nothing of that kind was suffered to remain in the house, nor was he ever permitted to go to any other, where such kind of furniture was in use. All this caution and art, instead of restraining, did but augment his passion. He had found means to get a little clavichord privately convey'd to a room at the top of the house. To this room he constantly stole when the family was asleep. He had made some progress before Music had been prohibited, and by his assiduous practice at the hours of rest, had made such farther advances, as, tho' not attended to at that time, were no flight prognoftics of his future greatnefs.

And here it may not be unpleafing to the reader, juft to remind him of the minute and furprifing refemblance between thefe paffages in the early periods of HANDEL's life, and fome which are recorded in that of the celebrated monfieur Pafcal †, written by his fifter. Nothing could equal the bias of the one to Mathematics, but the bias of the other to Mufic: both in their very childhood out-did the efforts of maturer age: they purfued their refpective ftudies not only without any affiftance, but againft the confent of their parents, and in fpite of all the oppofition they contrived to give them.

We

† Tycho Brahe is another inftance of the like kind.

We left our little traveller juſt on his arrival with his father at the Duke of Saxe-Weiſenfels. In ſuch a ſituation it was not eaſy to keep him from getting at harpſichords, and his father was too much engaged to watch him ſo cloſely there as he had done at home. He often mentioned to his friends, this uncontroulable humour of his ſon, which he told them he had taken great pains to ſubdue, but hitherto with little or no ſucceſs. He ſaid it was eaſy to foreſee, that if it was not ſubdued very ſoon, it would preclude all improvements in the ſcience for which he intended him, and wholly diſconcert the plan that had been formed and agreed on for his education.

The reaſonableneſs of ſuch apprehenſions every one admitted, in cafe it was determined to adhere to the fcheme above-mentioned. But the prudence of adhering to it was doubted by many. It was obferved with reafon, that where Nature feemed to declare herfelf in fo ftrong a manner, refiftance was often not only fruitlefs, but pernicious. Some faid, that, from all the accounts, the cafe appeared fo defperate, that nothing but the cutting off his fingers could prevent his playing; and others affirmed, that it was a pity any thing *fhould* prevent it. Such were the fentiments and declarations of the Doctor's friends in regard to his fon. It is not likely they would have had any great effect, but for the following incident, which gave their advice all the weight and authority it feems to have deferved.

It

It happened one morning, that while he was playing on the organ after the service was over, the Duke was in the church. Something there was in the manner of playing, which drew his attention so strongly, that his Highness, as soon as he returned, asked his valet de chambre who it was that he had heard at the organ, when the service was over. The valet replied, that it was his brother. The Duke demanded to see him.

After he had seen him, and made all the inquiries which it was natural for a man of taste and discernment to make on such an occasion, he told his physician, that every father must judge for himself in what manner to dispose of his children; but that, for his own part, he could not but consider it

as

as a sort of crime against the public and posterity, to rob the world of such a rising Genius!

The old Doctor still retained his prepossessions in favour of the Civil Law. Though he was convinced it was almost become an act of necessity to yield to his son's inclinations (as it seemed an act of duty to yield to the Prince's advice and authority) yet it was not without the utmost reluctance that he brought himself to this resolution. He was sensible of the Prince's goodness in taking such notice of his son, and giving his opinion concerning the best method of education. But he begged leave humbly to represent to his Highness, that though Music was an elegant art, and a fine amusement, yet if considered as an occupation, it had little dignity,

as

as having for its object nothing better than mere pleasure and entertainment: that whatever degree of eminence his son might arrive at in such a profession, he thought that a much less degree in many others would be far preferable.

The Prince could not agree with him in his notions of Music as a profession, which he said were much too low and disparaging, as great excellence in any kind entitled men to great honour. And as to profit, he observed how much more likely he would be to succeed, if suffered to pursue the path that Nature and Providence seemed to have marked out for him; than if he was forced into another track to which he had no such bias; nay, to which he had a direct aversion. He concluded with saying, that he was far
from

from recommending the ſtudy of Muſic in excluſion of the Languages, or of the Civil Law, provided it was poſſible to reconcile them together: what he wiſhed was, that all of them might have fair play; that no violence might be uſed, but the boy be left at liberty to follow the natural bent of his faculties, whatever that might be.

All this while he had kept his eyes ſtedfaſtly fixed on his powerful advocate; and his ears were as watchful and attentive to the impreſſions which the Prince's diſcourſe made upon his father.

The iſſue of their debate was this: not only a toleration was obtained for Muſic, but conſent for a maſter to be employed, who ſhould forward and aſſiſt him in his

his advances on his return to Hall. At his departure from Weisenfels, the Prince fill'd his pockets with money, and told him, with a smile, that if he minded his studies, no encouragements should be wanting.

The great civilities which he had received at the court of Weisenfels, the prosperous issue of the debate just mentioned, but especially the friendly and generous dismission which the Prince had given him, were often the subject of his thoughts. These fortunate incidents served to foment that native emulation, and to inflame that inbred ambition, which, even at this early period it was easy to discover in him.

The first thing which his father did at his return to Hall, was to place him under one ZACKAW, who
was

was organist to the cathedral church. This person had great abilities in his profession, and was not more qualified than inclined to do justice to any pupil of a hopeful disposition. HANDEL pleased him so much, that he never thought he could do enough for him. The first object of his attention was to ground him thoroughly in the principles of harmony. His next care was to cultivate his imagination, and form his taste. He had a large collection of Italian as well as German music: he shewed him the different styles of different nations; the excellences and defects of each particular author; and, that he might equally advance in the practical part, he frequently gave him subjects to work, and made him copy, and play, and compose in his stead. Thus he had more exercise, and

more

more experience than ufually falls to the fhare of any learner at his years.

ZACKAW was proud of a pupil, who already began to attract the attention of all perfons who lived near Hall, or reforted thither from diftant quarters. And he was glad of an affiftant, who, by his uncommon talents, was capable of fupplying his place, whenever he had an inclination to be abfent, as he often was, from his love of company, and a chearful glafs. It may feem ftrange to talk of an affiftant at feven years of age, for he could not be more, if indeed he was quite fo much, when firft he was committed to the care of this perfon. But it will appear much ftranger, that by the time
he

he was nine he began to compose the church service for voices and instruments, and from that time actually did compose a service every week for three years successively. However, it must not be forgot, that he had made some progress at home, before his father began to be alarmed, and, in consequence thereof, had forbid him to touch any musical instrument: that, after this severe prohibition, he had made further advances at stolen intervals by his practice on the clavichord; and after that had made the most of his moderate stay at the court of Weisenfels, where he found many instruments, and more admirers.

We have already hinted at some striking coincidencies of life and character, which are found in him,

and

and the famous Pascal. In this place we may just observe, that the latter, at the age of twelve compos'd a treatise on the propagation of sounds, and at sixteen another upon conic sections.

From the few facts just related it is easy to guess, that from the time of HANDEL's having a master in form, the Civil Law could have had no great share of his attention. The bent of his mind to Music was now so evident, and so prevailing, that the Prince's advice was punctually followed. No further endeavours were used to alter or correct it. The consequence of this full liberty was soon perceived, the pupil surpassed the master, the master himself confessed his superiority. HALL was not a place for so aspiring a youth to be long confined to. During this interval of three or four years, he had made all the improvements that were any way confiftent with the opportunities it afforded; but he was impatient for another fituation, which would afford him better, and fuch a one at length prefented itfelf. After fome confultations, BERLIN was the place agreed on. He had a friend and relation at that court, on whofe care and kindnefs his parents could rely. It was in the year 1698 that he went to Berlin. The Opera there was in a flourifhing condition, under the direction of the King of Pruffia, (grandfather of the prefent) who, by the encouragement which he gave to fingers and compofers, drew thither fome of the moft eminent from Italy, and other parts. Among thefe were BUONONCINI and

ATTILIO,

Attilio, the same who afterwards came to England while Handel was here, and of whom the former was at the head of a formidable oppofition againft him. This perfon was in high requeft for his compofitions, probably the beft which that court had known. But from his natural temper, he was eafily elated with fuccefs, and apt to be intoxicated with admiration and applaufe. Though Handel was talk'd of as a moft extraordinary player on the harpfichord for one fo young, yet on account of his years he had always confidered him as a mere child. But as people ftill perfifted in their encomiums, it was his fancy to try the truth of them. For this end he compofed a Cantata in the chromatic ftyle, difficult in every refpect, and fuch as even a mafter, he thought, would be puzzled to play, or accompany without some previous practice. When he found that he, whom he had regarded as a mere child, treated this formidable composition as a mere trifle, not only executing it at sight, but with a degree of accuracy, truth, and expression hardly to be expected even from repeated practice;— then indeed he began to see him in another light, and to talk of him in another tone.

Attilio, somewhat his inferior as a composer, was a better performer on the harpsichord, and, from the sweetness of his temper, and modesty of his character, was much more beloved as a man. His fondness for Handel commenced at his first coming to Berlin, and continued to the time of his leaving it.

He

He would often take him on his knee, and make him play on his harpfichord for an hour together, equally pleafed and furprized with the extraordinary proficiency of fo young a perfon; for at this time he could not exceed thirteen, as may eafily be feen by comparing dates. The kindnefs of ATTILIO was not thrown away; as he was always welcome, he never loft any opportunity of being with him, or of learning from him all that a perfon of his age and experience was capable of fhewing him. It would be injuftice to BUONONCINI not to mention his civilities to HAN-DEL, but they were accompanied with that kind of diftance and referve, which always leffen the value of an obligation, by the very endeavour to enhance it. The age of the perfon to be obliged seems to remove all suspicion of rivalship or jealousy. One so young could hardly be the object of either; and yet from what afterwards happened, such a notion may appear to some persons not altogether destitute of probability. Those who are fond of explaining former passages by subsequent events, would be apt to say, that the seeds of enmity were sown at Berlin; and that though they did not appear 'till the scene was changed, they waited only for time and occasion to produce them.

Thus much is certain, that the little stranger had not been long at court before his abilities became known to the King, who frequently sent for him, and made him large presents. Indeed his Majesty, convinc'd of his singular
endow-

endowments, and unwilling to lose the opportunity of patronizing so rare a genius, had conceived a design of cultivating it at his own expence. His intention was to send him to Italy, where he might be formed under the best masters, and have opportunities of hearing and seeing all that was excellent in the kind. As soon as it was intimated to HANDEL's friends (for he was yet too young to determine for himself) they deliberated what answer it would be proper to return, in case this scheme should be proposed in form. It was the opinion of many that his fortune was already made, and that his relations would certainly embrace such an offer with the utmost alacrity. Others, who better understood the temper and spirit of the court at Berlin, thought this

this a matter of nice fpeculation, and cautious debate. For they well knew, that if he once engag'd in the King's fervice, he muſt remain in it, whether he liked it, or not; that if he continued to pleafe, it would be a reafon for not parting with him; and that if he happened to difpleafe, his ruin would be the certain confequence. To accept an offer of this nature, was the fame thing as to enter into a formal engagement, but how to refufe it was ftill the difficulty. At length it was refolved that fome excufe muſt be found. It was not long before the King caufed his intentions to be fignified, and the anfwer was, that the Doctor would always retain the profoundeſt fenfe of the honour done to him by the notice which his Majefty had been gracioufly pleafed to take of his
fon;

son; but as he himself was now grown old, and could not expect to have him long with him, he humbly hoped the King would forgive his defire to decline the offer which had been made him by order of his Majefty.

I am not able to inform the reader how this anfwer was relifhed by the King, whom we may fuppofe not much accuftomed to refufals, efpecially of this fort. Such an incident made it improper for HANDEL to ftay much longer at the court of Berlin, where the more his abilities fhould be known and commended, the more fome perfons would be apt to fift and fcrutinize the motives of his father's conduct.

Many and great were the compliments and civilities which he received on his leaving Berlin. As yet he had been but twice from home; and both times had received such marks of honour and diftinction, as are seldom, if ever, paid to one of his age and condition. On his return to Hall, he began to feel himself more, to be confcious of his own fuperiority, to difcover that fpirit of emulation, and paffion for fame, which urged him ftrongly to go out into the world, and try what fuccefs he fhould have in it. His acquaintance with the eminent mafters at Berlin had opened his mind to new ideas of excellence, and fhewn him in a more extended view the perfections of his art. After his friends had refufed fuch offers as the King had made him, he never

could

could endure the thought of ſtaying long at home, either as a pupil or ſubſtitute to his old maſter ZACKAW. He had heard ſo high a character of the ſingers and compoſers of Italy, that his thoughts ran much on a journey into that country. But this project required a longer purſe than he was as yet provided with, and was therefore ſuſpended till ſuch time as it could be compaſſed without hazard or inconvenience. In the mean while, as his fortune was to depend on his ſkill in his profeſſion, it was neceſſary to conſider of ſome place leſs diſtant, where he might employ his time to advantage, and be ſtill improving in knowledge and experience. Next to the Opera of Berlin, that of HAMBURGH was in the higheſt requeſt. It was reſolved folved to fend him thither on his own bottom, and chiefly with a view to improvement. It was a wife refolution not to engage him too early with a view to profit. How many parents have murdered the fine talents of their children by weakly facrificing that liberty and independency, which are effential to their exertion! This confideration had ever been attended to by his friends while he was under their direction. And it is very remarkable that HANDEL, when he came to act for himfelf, conftantly purfued the fame falutary maxim. In the fequel of his life he refufed the higheft offers from perfons of the greateft diftinction; nay, the higheft favours from the faireft of the fex, only becaufe he would not be cramped or confined by particular attachments.

His father's death happened not long after his return from Berlin. This event produced a confiderable change for the worfe in the income of his mother. That he might not add to her expences, the firft thing which he did on his arrival at Hamburgh, was to procure fcholars, and obtain fome employment in the orcheftra. Such was his induftry and fuccefs in fetting out, that the firft remittance which his mother fent him he generoufly returned her, accompanied with a fmall prefent of his own. On this occafion it is but juftice to obferve, that the fame generous regard for thofe with whom he had any natural or accidental

dental connection, appeared in the later, as well as in the earlier periods of his life. But a very few years before his death, being informed that the widow of Zackaw was left ill provided for, he sent her money more than once. He would have done the same by her son, for whose welfare he appeared to be equally anxious; but the assurances he received, that all such services would only furnish him with opportunities of increasing those sottish habits he had contracted, with-held his hand.

Before we advance any farther in his history, it is necessary some accounts should be given of the Opera at Hamburgh, as well as some character of the composer and singers.

The

The principal fingers were CON-RATINI and MATHYSON. The latter was secretary to Sir Cyril Wych, who was resident for the English court, had HANDEL for his musicmaster, and was himself a fine player on the harpsichord. MATHYSON was no great singer, for which reason he sung only occasionally; but he was a good actor, a good composer of lessons, and a good player on the harpsichord. He wrote and translated several treatises. One that he wrote was on Composition. He had thoughts of writing the life of HANDEL many years before his death. Had he pursued this design, he would have had advantages beyond what we can pretend to, *i. e.* ampler and fresher materials; at least, for so much of the life as had then elapsed. All that
is

is here intended, is to give a plain, artless account of such particulars as we have been able to learn, and such only as we have reason to believe authentic. To return to our narration.

CONRATINI excelled greatly both as an actress and a singer. KEYSAR did the same as a composer, but being a man of gaiety and expence, involved himself in debts, which forced him to abscond. His Operas, for some time, continued to be performed during his absence. On his disappearing, the person who before had played the second harpsichord, demanded the first. This occasioned a dispute between him and HANDEL, the particulars of which, partly for the sake of their singularity, and partly on account

count of their importance, may deserve to be mentioned.

On what reasons Handel grounded his claim to the first harpsichord I do not understand: he had played a violin in the orchestra, he had a good command on this instrument, and was known to have a better on the other. But the older candidate was not unfit for the office, and insisted on the right of succession. Handel seemed to to have no plea but that of natural superiority, of which he was conscious, and from which he would not recede. This dispute occasioned parties in the Opera-house. On the one side it was said, with great appearance of reason, that to set such a boy as Handel over a person so much his senior, was both unjust and unprecedented.

On the other, it was urged with some plausibility, that the Opera was not to be ruined for punctilios; that it was easy to foresee, from the difficulties KEYSAR was under, that a Composer would soon be wanted, but not so easy to find a person capable of succeeding him, unless it were HANDEL. In short, matters (they said) were now at that pass, that the question, if fairly stated, was not who should conduct the Opera, but whether there should be any Opera at all.

These arguments prevailed; and he, to whom the first place seemed of course to be due, was constrained to yield it to his stripling-competitor. But how much he felt the indignity, may be guessed from the nature and degree of his resentment; more suited to the glowing
temper

temper of an Italian, than to the phlegmatic conſtitution of a German: For, determined to make HANDEL pay dear for his priority, he ſtifled his rage for the preſent, only to wait an opportunity of giving it full vent. As they were coming out of the orcheſtra, he made a puſh at him with a ſword, which being aimed full at his heart, would for ever have removed him from the office he had uſurped, but for the friendly *Score*, which he accidentally carried in his boſom; and through which to have forced it, would have demanded all the might of Ajax himſelf.

Had this happened in the early ages, not a mortal but would have been perſuaded that APOLLO himſelf had interpofed to preferve him, in the form of a mufic-book.

From the circumftances which are related of this affair, it has more the appearance of an affaffination, than of a rencounter: if the latter, one of HANDEL's years might well be wanting in the courage, or the fkill to defend himfelf: if the former, fuppofing him capable of making a defence, he could not be prepared for it.

How many great men, in the very dawning of their glory, have been planted, like him, on the very verge of deftruction! as if Fortune, jealous of Nature, made a fhew of facrificing her nobleft productions, only to remind her of that fupremacy to which fhe afpires!

Whatever

Whatever might be the merits of the quarrel at first, HANDEL seemed now to have purchased his title to precedence by the dangers he had incurred to support it. What he and his friends expected, soon happened. From conducting the performance, he became Composer to the Opera. KEYSAR, from his unhappy situation, could no longer supply the Manager, who therefore applied to HANDEL, and furnished him with a drama to set. The name of it was ALMERIA, and this was the first Opera which he made. The success of it was so great, that it ran for thirty nights without interruption. He was at this time not much above fourteen: before he was quite fifteen, he made a second, entitled FLORINDA; and soon after, a third called NERONE, which were heard with the same applause. It never was his intention to settle at Hamburgh: he told the Manager, on his first application to him, that he came thither only as a traveller, and with a view to improvement: that till the Compofer fhould be at liberty, or till fome other fucceffor or fubftitute could be found, he was willing to be employed, but was refolved to fee more of the world before he entered into any engagements, which would confine him long to any particular place. The Manager left that matter for him and his friends to determine; but fo long as he thought proper to be concerned in the Opera, he promifed him advantages at leaft as great as any Compofer that had gone before him. This indeed was no more than what intereft would readily fuggeft to a perfon in his fituation: for good houfes will always afford

good

good pay, to all who bear a part in the performance; and especially to that person, whose character and abilities can ensure its success.

At the time that ALMERIA and FLORINDA were performed, there were many persons of note at Hamburgh, among whom was the Prince of Tuscany, brother to John Gaston de Medicis, Grand Duke. The Prince was a great lover of the art for which his country is so renowned. HANDEL's proficiency in it, not only procured him access to his Highness, but occasioned a sort of intimacy betwixt them: they frequently discoursed together on the state of Music in general, and on the merits of Composers, Singers, and Performers in particular. The Prince would often lament that HANDEL was not acquainted with those of Italy;

shewed

shewed him a large collection of Italian Music; and was very desirous he should return with him to Florence. HANDEL plainly confessed that he could see nothing in the Music which answered the high character his Highness had given it. On the contrary, he thought it so very indifferent, that the Singers, he said, must be angels to recommend it. The Prince smiled at the severity of his censure, and added, that there needed nothing but a journey to Italy to reconcile him to the style and taste which prevailed there. He assured him that there was no country in which a young proficient could spend his time to so much advantage; or in which every branch of his profession was cultivated with so much care. HANDEL replied, that if this were so, he was much at a loss to conceive

how

how such great culture should be followed by so little fruit. However, what his Highness had told him, and what he had before heard of the fame of the Italians, would certainly induce him to undertake the journey he had been pleased to recommend, the moment it should be convenient. The Prince then intimated, that if he chose to return with him, no conveniences should be wanting. HANDEL, without intending to accept of the favour designed him, expressed his sense of the honour done him. For he resolved to go to Italy on his own bottom, as soon as he could make a purse for that occasion. This noble spirit of independency, which possessed him almost from his childhood, was never known to forsake him, not even in the most distressful seasons of his life.

During

During his continuance at Hamburgh, he made a confiderable number of Sonatas. But what became of thefe pieces he never could learn, having been fo imprudent as to let them go out of his hands.

Four or five years had elapfed from the time of his coming to Hamburgh, to that of his leaving it.. It has already been obferved, that inftead of being chargeable to his mother, he began to be ferviceable to her before he was well fettled in his new fituation. Tho' he had continued to fend her remittances from time to time, yet, clear of his own expences, he had made up a purfe of 200 ducats. On the ftrength of this fund he refolved to fet out for Italy.

The

The number of fchools and academies for Mufic fubfifting in the different quarters of this country, and the vaft encouragements afforded to thofe who excel in the Art, have long confpired, with all the advantages of conftitution and climate, to render it the moft eminent part of the worldfor its Compofers, Singers, and Performers. As each of thefe feparate claffes hath a ftyle and manner peculiar to itfelf, fo there are fome things well worth obferving, which are common to them all. And a foreigner, who would make a figure in the profeffion, ought to obferve them with the greater exactnefs, becaufe they are fuch as cannot be marked, or written, or even defcribed. So little are they to be learnt by rule, that they are not unfrequently direct
viola-

violations * of rule. I am at a loss what to call them, unless they are certain beauties and delicacies in *sentiment* and *expression*, which are only to be catched from long habit, and attentive observation. Tho' they seem, at first sight, to be next to nothing, yet how much depends upon

* The very first answer of the Fugue in the overture for Mucius Scævola, affords an instance of this kind. Geminiani, the strictest observer of rule, was so charmed with this direct transgression of it, that, on hearing its effect, he cried out, Quel semitono (meaning the f. sharp) vale un mondo!

The younger Scarlatti often makes a happy use of these licences, though some think he uses them too often. It is certain that they ought not to be used without great caution and judgment. They would not be tolerated but for those great and striking effects which they are found to produce, when under the management of a great Master.

It is needless to observe the exact analogy which Poetry and Painting bear to Music in respect to these licences, to which the slender company of great Genius's seem to claim an exclusive privilege.

upon them, we may judge from the terms in which the Italians usually describe them, viz. *è quel tantino, chi fa tutto.*

Indeed, from the best information which we can get of the state of the Art in its different stages and periods, it should seem as if no people ever attained to such excellency in Vocal Music, or possessed so extensive a command over the passions and affections as the Italians.†

The

---

† Here I am sensible that I have the ABBE DU BOS directly against me. So strong are his prejudices in favour of the Music of his own nation, that he makes no scruple of setting LULLI above all the Italian Masters. Vossius having declared his reasons for preferring the ancient to the modern Musicians; and the ABBE not conceivng any of either class fit to be compared with his countryman, desires his readers to consider the question in the following view:

"Qu'on se figure donc quelle comparaison Vossius auroit faite des CANTATES, & des SO-

NATES

The paſſionate admirers of HANDEL's ſtyle, are apt to confound this characteriſtic excellence of *theirs* with

NATES des Italiens, avec les Symphonies & les Recits de LULLI, s'il les eût connus, lorſqu'il écrivit le livre dont je parle."

And might we not aſk the ABBE DU BOS what he conceives that the ſame learned Critic would have thought on this ſubject, had he lived to ſee the very elegant and ſenſible *Lettre ſur la Muſique Françoiſe* [par J. J. Rouſſeau, Citoyen de Genéve] in which it is proved, almoſt to a demonſtration, as well from the intractable genius of the language, as from the perverted taſte of the nation, that the French are never likely to have any Muſic which an impartial and competent judge of the Art would endure. This is ſo true, that what is tolerable in LULLI himſelf, is borrowed from thoſe very Italians ſo lightly valued. The advantages which he drew from his acquaintance with CORELLI, will not be forgot, any more than the return which he made him by raiſing a faction againſt him, and driving him from Paris. Theſe are no good arguments of the greatneſs of his mind, notwithſtanding he was thought worthy of being exalted to the rank of a Stateſman and Privy-counſellor.

with that effeminacy of taste, which proceeds from the vain attempt to command those strong feelings of the soul without genius, art, or judgment. They do not consider the advantages he derived from his thorough acquaintance with the Italian

After all that is here insinuated to his disadvantage as a Musician, I am far from thinking that he was destitute of talents, and less reason is there for believing this of his great successor Monsieur RAMEAU. It is the more to be lamented that fortune should have thrown them where the best parts which nature could bestow would be sure of receiving a wrong biass; as well from the untoward cast of the language (equally unfit both for Music and Poetry) as from the corruption of the national taste, to whatever ulterior causes this latter may be ascribed.

'Tis true, Mr. ADDISON, at the end of his last paper upon Operas, has not only vindicated, but commended the taste of the French for Music. But in vain does the ingenious ABBE endeavour to avail himself of his authority. For though all men will agree with him that the Music of every country should be

(48)

Italian Masters, to whose delicate and beautiful melody he added indeed still higher touches of expression, at the same time that he united it with the full strong harmony of his own country. †

We

be adapted, as fas as may be, to the pronunciation and accent of its inhabitants; yet doth it by no means follow, that the pronunciation and accent of every people is equally suited to the purposes of Music; the unalterable principles of which, nay, those of Architecture and Painting also, he resolves at once into the inconstant, arbitrary decisions of custom and caprice. See Spect. Vol. I. N°. 29. p. 121. 12mo Edit. The excellence of Mr. ADDISON both as a man and a writer, hath almost consecrated his mistakes; and the influence of his judgment in the present case is the more to be feared, because it is much better known, that he had an exceeding fine taste for the polite arts in general, than that he had a very imperfect knowledge of Music in particular; yet the poetry in his Opera of ROSAMOND is as strong a proof of this, as his idea of the French compositions.

† A more particular account of the Italian Music is given in the beginning of the observations subjoined to the life.

We left him juſt on the point of his removal to Italy; where he arrived ſoon after the Prince of Tuſcany. FLORENCE, as it is natural to ſuppoſe, was his firſt deſtination; for he was too well known to his Highneſs to need any other recommendations at the court of the Grand Duke, to whoſe palace he had free acceſs at all ſeaſons, and whoſe kindneſs he experienced on all occaſions. The fame of his abilities had raiſed the curioſity of the Duke and his court, and rendered them very impatient to have ſome performance of his compoſing. With leſs experience, and fewer years to mature his judgment, he had hitherto ſucceeded to the utmoſt extent of his wiſhes. But he was now to be brought to the trial in a ſtrange country, where

the ftyle was as different from that of his own nation, as the manners and cuftoms of the Italians are from thofe of the Germans. Senfible as he was of this difadvantage, his ambition would not fuffer him to decline the trial to which he was invited. At the age of eighteen he made the Opera of RODRIGO, for which he was prefented with 100 fequins, and a fervice of plate. This may ferve for a fufficient teftimony of its favourable reception. VITTORIA, who was much admired both as an Actrefs, and a Singer, bore a principal part in this Opera. She was a fine woman, and had for fome time been much in the good graces of his Serene Highnefs. But, from the natural reftlefnefs of certain hearts, fo little fenfible was fhe of her exalted fituation, that fhe conceived a defign of transferring
her

her affections to another person. HANDEL's youth and comeliness, joined with his fame and abilities in Music, had made impressions on her heart. Tho' she had the art to conceal them for the present, she had not perhaps the power, certainly not the intention, to efface them.

The nature of his design in travelling made it improper for him to stay long in any one place. He had stayed near a year at Florence, and it was his resolution to visit every part of Italy, which was any way famous for its musical performances. VENICE was his next resort. He was first discovered there at a Masquerade, while he was playing on a harpsichord in his visor. SCARLATTI happened to be there, and affirmed that it could be no one but the famous Saxon, or the devil. Being thus detected, he was strongly importuned to compose an Opera. But there was so little prospect of either honour or advantage from such an undertaking, that he was very unwilling to engage in it. At last, however, he consented, and in three weeks he finished his AGRIPPINA, which was performed twenty-seven nights successively; and in a theatre which had been shut up for a long time, notwithstanding there were two other Opera-houses open at the same time; at one of which GASPARINI presided, as LOTTI did at the other. The audience was so enchanted with this performance, that a stranger who should have seen the manner in which they were affected, would have imagined they had all been distracted.

The

The theatre, at almoſt every pauſe, reſounded with ſhouts and acclamations of *viva il caro Saſſone!* and other expreſſions of approbation too extravagant to be mentioned. They were thunderſtruck with the grandeur and ſublimity of his ſtile: for never had they known till then all the powers of harmony and modulation ſo cloſely arrayed, and ſo forcibly combined.

This Opera * drew over all the beſt ſingers from the other houſes. Among the foremoſt of theſe was the famous VITTORIA, who a little before HANDEL's removal to Venice

---

* It ſeems that French Horns, and other wind-inſtruments as little known to the *Italians*, were introduced on this occaſion. I believe they never had heard them before, as accompaniments to the voice.

nice had obtained permission of the grand Duke to sing in one of the houses there. At AGRIPPINA her inclinations gave new lustre to her talents. HANDEL seemed almost as great and majestic as APOLLO, and it was far from the lady's intention to be so cruel and obstinate as DAPHNE.

Having mentioned the most material occurrences at Venice, we are now to relate his reception at ROME. The fame of his musical atchievements at Florence and at Venice had reached that metropolis long before him. His arrival therefore was immediately known, and occasioned civil enquiries and polite messages from persons of the first distinction there. Among his greatest admirers was the Cardinal OTTOBONI, a person of a refined taste,

taſte, and princely magnificence. Beſides a fine collection of pictures and ſtatues, he had a large library of Muſic, and an excellent band of performers, which he kept in conſtant pay. The illuſtrious Corelli played the firſt violin, and had apartments in the Cardinal's palace. It was a cuſtomary thing with his eminence to have performances of Operas, Oratorios, and ſuch other grand compoſitions, as could from time to time be procured. Handel was deſired to furniſh his quota; and there was always ſuch a greatneſs and ſuperiority in the pieces compoſed by him, as rendered thoſe of the beſt maſters comparatively little and inſignificant. There was alſo ſomething in his manner ſo very different from what the Italians had been uſed to, that thoſe who were seldom or never at a loss in performing any other Music, were frequently puzzled how to execute his. Corelli himself complained of the difficulty he found in playing his Overtures. Indeed there was in the whole cast of these compositions, but especially in the opening of them, such a degree of fire and force, as never could confort with the mild graces, and placid elegancies of a genius so totally dissimilar. Several fruitless attempts Handel had one day made to instruct him in the manner of executing these spirited passages. Piqued at the tameness with which he still played them, he snatches the instrument out of his hand; and, to convince him how little he understood them, played the passages himself. But Corelli, who was a person of great modesty

and

and meekness, wanted no conviction of this sort; for he ingenuously declared that he did not understand them; *i. e.* knew not how to execute them properly, and give them the strength and expression they required. When HANDEL appeared impatient, *Ma, caro Saffone* (said he) *questa Musica è nel stylo Francese, di ch' io non m' intendo* *.

A little incident relating to CORELLI, shews his character so strongly, that I shall be excused for reciting it, though foreign to our present purpose. He was requested one evening to play, to a large and polite company, a fine Solo which he

* The Overture for IL TRIONFO DEL TEMPO was that which occasioned CORELLI the greatest difficulty. At his desire therefore he made a symphony in the room of it, more in the Italian style.

he had lately compofed. Juft as he was in the midft of his performance, fome of the number began to difcourfe together a little unfeafonably; Corelli gently lays down his inftrument. Being afked whether any thing was the matter with him? Nothing, he replied, he was only afraid that he interrupted converfation. The elegant propriety of this filent cenfure, joined with his genteel and good-humoured anfwer, afforded great pleafure, even to the perfons who occafioned it. They begged him to refume his inftrument, affuring him at the fame time, that he might depend on all the attention, which the occafion required, and which his merit ought before to have commanded.

Hitherto Handel has chiefly been confidered, if not wholly, in the

the quality of Compofer. We fhall now have occafion to enter into his character as a Player or Performer. And it muft not be forgot, that, though he was well acquainted with the nature and management of the violin; yet his chief practice, and greateft maftery was on the organ and harpfichord.

When he came firft into Italy, the mafters in greateft efteem were ALESSANDRO SCARLATTI, GASPARINI, and LOTTI. The † firft of thefe he became acquainted with at Cardinal OTTOBONI's. Here alfo he became known to DOMINICO SCARLATTI, now living in Spain, and author of the celebrated leffons.

† This perfon (*i. e.* the elder SCARLATTI) was author of an Opera entitled, PRINCIPESSA FIDELE, which is reckoned a chéf-d'oeuvre in its kind. He alfo made feveral Cantatas very highly efteemed by the judges of Mufic.

fons. As he was an exquifite player on the harpfichord, the Cardinal was refolved to bring him and HANDEL together for a trial of fkill. The iffue of the trial on the harpfichord hath been differently reported. It has been faid that fome gave the preference to SCARLATTI. However, when they came to the Organ there was not the leaft pretence for doubting to which of them it belonged. SCARLATTI himfelf declared the fuperiority of his antagonift, and owned ingenuoufly, that till he had heard him upon this inftrument, he had no conception of its powers. So greatly was he ftruck with his peculiar method of playing, that he followed him all over Italy, and was never fo happy as when he was with him.

HANDEL used often to speak of this person with great satisfaction; and indeed there was reason for it; for besides his great talents as an artist, he had the sweetest temper, and the genteelest behaviour. On the other hand, it was mentioned but lately by the two PLAS [the famous Haut-bois] who came from Madrid, that SCARLATTI, as oft as he was admired for his great execution, would mention HANDEL, and cross himself in token of veneration.

Though no two persons ever arrived at such perfection on their respective instruments, yet it is remarkable that there was a total difference in their manner. The characteristic excellence of SCAR-
LATTI

LATTI seems to have consisted in a certain elegance and delicacy of expression. HANDEL had an uncommon brilliancy and command of finger: but what distinguished him from all other players who possessed these same qualities, was that amazing fulness, force, and energy, which he joined with them. And this observation may be applied with as much justness to his compositions, as to his playing.

While he was at Rome he was also much and often at the palaces of the two Cardinals, COLONNA, and PAMPHILII. The latter had some talents for Poetry, and wrote the drama of IL TRIONFO DEL TEMPO, besides several other pieces, which HANDEL set at his desire, some in the compass of a single evening, and

and others extempore. † One of these was in honour of HANDEL himself. He was compared to ORPHEUS, and exalted above the rank of mortals. Whether his Eminence chose this subject as most likely to inspire him with fine conceptions, or with a view to discover how far so great an Artist was proof against the assaults of vanity, it is not material to determine. HANDEL's modesty was not however so excessive, as to hinder him from

com-

---

† The ABBE DU BOS, speaking of that general turn for Music for which the Italians from the highest to the lowest have ever been remarkable, continues thus,— Ils sçavent encore chanter leurs amours dans des vers qu'ils composent sur le champ, & qu'ils accompagnent du son de leurs instruments. Ils les touchent, si non avec délicatesse, du moins avec assez de justesse: c'est ce qui s'apelle *improviser*.

complying with the defire of his illuftrious * friend.

As he was familiar with fo many of the Sacred Order, and of a perfuafion fo totally repugnant to theirs, it is natural to imagine that fome of them would expoftulate with him on that fubject. For how could thefe good catholicks be fuppofed to bear him any real regard, without endeavouring to lead him out of the road to damnation? Being preffed very clofely on this article by one of thefe exalted Ecclefiaftics, he replied, that he was neither qualified, nor difpofed to enter into enquiries of this fort, but was refolved to die a member of that communion, whether true or falfe, in which he was born and bred. No hopes appearing

* This expreffion will not be thought too ftrong by thofe who know what fincere efteem and cordial regard he attracted from perfons of the higheft diftinction.

pearing of a real converſion, the next attempt was to win him over to outward conformity. But neither arguments, nor offers had any effect, unleſs it were that of confirming him ſtill more in the principles of proteſtantiſm. Theſe applications were made only by a few perſons. The generality looked upon him as a man of honeſt, though miſtaken principles, and therefore concluded that he would not eaſily be induced to change them. While he was at Rome he made a kind of Oratorio entitled, RESURRECTIONE, and one hundred and fifty Cantatas, beſides Sonatas and other Muſic.

From Rome he removed to NAPLES, where, as at moſt other places, he had a palazzo at command, and was provided with table, coach, and all other accommodations.

tions. While he was at this capital, he made ACIS and GALATEA, the words Italian, and the Mufic different from ours. It was compofed at the requeft of DONNA LAURA, whether a Portugueze or a Spanifh Princefs, I will not be certain. But the pomp and magnificence of this lady fhould feem to fpeak her of Spanifh extraction. For fhe lived, acted, and converfed with a ftate truly regal.

How HANDEL executed his tafk, we may guefs from what he has fince produced on the fame and other fubjects, under all the difadvantages of a language lefs foft and fonorous, and of Dramas conftructed without art or judgment, order or confiftency.

While he was at Naples he received invitations from moft of the

prin-

principal perfons who lived within reach of that capital; and lucky was he efteemed, who could engage him foonest, and detain him longest. After he quitted Naples, he made a fecond vifit to Florence, Rome, and Venice. Meeting with many of his friends, he made fome ftay at each of thofe places. The whole time of his abode in Italy was fix years. During this interval he had made abundance of Mufic, and fome in almoft every fpecies of compofition. Thefe early fruits of his ftudies would doubtlefs be vaft curiofities could they now be met with. The lovers of the art would regard them with fomething of the fame veneration, which the Literati would pay to the precious remains of a LIVY, a CÆSAR, or a TACITUS! Indeed the few fragments of thofe pieces which have come to our hands, serve only to increase our concern for the parts which have perished. And when the Reader is informed, that the two first Movements of Handel's seventh Suite in the 1st Vol. of his Lessons formerly stood for the Overture in his famous Opera of Agrippina; he will be less surprised at the extravagant admiration of a Venetian audience, than at this effort of his genius before he was well nineteen. From such a specimen, he will form some judgment of the work itself: he will be the more anxious for his other juvenile productions, some of which are probably lost, and the rest only to be met with among the few Virtuosi, whose enthusiastic veneration for all that is truly great and excellent in its kind, hath acquired them that title; and of whom it is difficult

cult to say, whether they are more active and indefatigable in the search of such treasure, or more careful and vigilant in the guarding of it.

Handel having now been long enough in Italy effectually to answer the purpose of his going thither, began to think of returning to his native country. Not that he intended this to be the end of his travels; for his curiosity was not yet allay'd, nor likely to be so while there was any musical court which he had not seen. Hanover was the first he stopped at. Steffani was there, and had met with favour and encouragement equal, if possible, to his singular desert. This person (whose character is elegantly sketched by a lover of his Art and friend to his memory) he had seen at Venice, the place of his nativity. Such an acquaintance he was glad to renew: for STEFFANI's compositions were excellent; his temper was exceedingly amiable; and his behaviour polite and genteel. Those who are inclined to see a fuller account of him, may consult those Memoirs of his Life, consisting indeed of a very few pages, but sufficient to do him great honour. We shall soon have occasion to mention him again, and therefore shall only add at present, that he was Master of the Chapel to his late MAJESTY, when he was only Elector of Hanover. This was an office and title highly creditable there, tho' far inferior to those which he afterwards bore.

At Hanover there was also a Nobleman who had taken great notice

tice of HANDEL in Italy, and who did him great service (as will appear soon) when he came to ENGLAND for the second time. This person was Baron KILMANSECK. He introduced him at court, and so well recommended him to his Electoral Highness, that he immediately offered him a pension of 1500 Crowns per annum as an inducement to stay. Tho' such an offer from a Prince of his character was not to be neglected, HANDEL loved liberty too well to accept it hastily, and without reserve. He told the Baron how much he owed to his kind and effectual recommendation, as well as to his Highness's goodness and generosity. But he also expressed his apprehensions that the favour intended him would hardly be consistent either with the promise he had actually made to vifit the court of the Elector Palatine, or with the resolution he had long taken to pass over into England, for the sake of seeing that of LONDON.†. Upon this objection, the Baron consulted his Highness's pleasure, and HANDEL was then acquainted, that neither his promise nor his resolution should be superseded by his acceptance of the pension proposed. He had leave to be absent for a twelve-month or more, if he chose it; and to go whithersoever he pleased. On these easy conditions he thankfully accepted it.

To this handsome pension the place of Chapel-master was soon after added, on the voluntary resignation

of

---

† It seems he had received strong invitations to England from the Duke of Manchester.

of STEFFANI. He thought such an office not perfectly consistent with the high titles of Bishop and Ambassador, with which he was now invested. And he was glad of this, or any other opportunity of obliging HANDEL. Notwithstanding the new favour conferred upon him, he was still in possession of the privilege before allowed him, to perform his engagements, and pursue his travels. He considered it as his first and principal engagement to pay a visit to his Mother at Hall. Her extreme old-age, and total blindness, tho' they promised him but a melancholy interview, rendered this instance of his duty and regard the more necessary. When he had paid his respects to his relations and friends (among whom his old Master ZACKAW was by no means forgot)

got) he set out for DUSSELDORP. The Elector Palatine was much pleased with the punctual performance of his promise, but as much disappointed to find that he was engaged elsewhere. At parting he made him a present of a fine set of wrought plate for a desert, and in such a manner as added greatly to its value.

From Dusseldorp he made the best of his way through HOLLAND and embarqued for ENGLAND. It was in the winter of the year 1710, when he arrived at LONDON, one of the most memorable years of that longest, but most prosperous war (next to the present) which England had ever waged with a foreign power. For during this period scarce a mail arrived from Holland,
which

which did not bring some fresh account of victories or advantages gained by the English Hero over the armies of a Monarch, but lately the terror of Europe, tho' now the scorn of every Dutch Burgomaster. Nothing indeed seemed wanting to compleat the national felicity, but a person capable of charming down, by the magic of his melody, that evil spirit of faction and party, which fortune seems, at this time, to have conjured up, as it were in pure pity to her former favourite, the afflicted LEWIS! But HANDEL, great as he was, could not do for England, what David did for Saul. The same spirit which had so often appeared in the course of the war, presided at the congress for peace. The Music which HANDEL composed on the completion of it, will be be mentioned elsewhere. In the mean time, it may not be amiss to say a word or two on the state of Music at this his first coming into England.

Excepting a few good compositions in the church style, and of a very old date, I am afraid there was little to boast of, which we could call our own. At this time Operas were a sort of new acquaintance, but began to be established in the affections of the Nobility, many of whom had heard and admired performances of this kind in the country which gave them birth. But the conduct of them here, *i. e.* all that regards the drama, or plan, including also the machinery, scenes, and decorations, was foolish and absurd almost beyond imagination.

The

The laſt Pope but one was ſo exceedingly entertained with Mr. Addison's humourous account of this curious management, that on reading his papers relating to it, he laughed till he ſhook his ſides. Mr. Addison ſeems, a little unfairly, to impute this vitiated taſte to the growing fondneſs for every thing that was Italian. It is far from impoſſible, that the Manager might have found this taſte eſtabliſhed here, and have been obliged to conform to it. Who or what the Compoſers were, we are not informed; nor is it very material to enquire. For, from the account of the commencement of the Italian Opera here, as we find it in the 18th Nº of the Spectator, it is plain, that, what with the confuſion of languages, and the tranſpoſition of
paſſions

paffions and fentiments owing to that caufe, the beft Compofer could hardly be diftinguifhed from the worft. The arrival of HANDEL put an end to this reign of nonfenfe.

The report of his uncommon abilities had been conveyed to England before his arrival, and through various channels. Some perfons here had feen him in Italy, and others during his refidence at Hanover. He was foon introduced at Court, and honoured with marks of the Queen's favour. Many of the nobility were impatient for an Opera of his compofing. To gratify this eagernefs, RINALDO, the firft he made in England, was finifhed in a fortnight's time. The words of the Opera are by ROSSI, the firft
fen-

sentence of whose preface is quoted by the Spectator. This contains a sort of panegyric on his own poetry, for which however he has soon after the modesty to make an apology. As it is somewhat curious, I shall present the reader with a little specimen of it.

" Gradisci, ti prego, discretto lettore, questa mia rapida fatica, e se non merita le tue lodi, almeno non privarla del tuo compatimento, chi dirò più tosto giustizia per un tempo così ristretto: poiche il Signer HENDEL, Orfeo del nostro secolo, nel porla in Musica, a pena mi diede tempo di scrivere; e viddi, con mio grande stupore, in due sole settimane armonizata al maggior grado di perfezzione un Opera intiera."

The subject-matter of this Opera was furnished to Rossi by the late Mr. Aaron Hill, who also gave the publick an English version of it. We learn from his preface, that at this time the Theatre at the Hay-Market was under his direction. And it appears from the account of his life prefixed to the last edition of his dramatic works, that the year before he was manager of that at Drury-Lane. The character of this person seems to have been almost as singular as his adventures. Born of a good family, and endowed with some natural talents, he might perhaps have arrived at that eminence to which he aspired, could he have confined himself to any single pursuit. But he was one of those active and enterprising spirits, that attempt every thing, and, for want of discerning their proper province, bring nothing to perfection. He travelled much, read much, and wrote much; and all, as it should seem, to very little purpose. His intimate acquaintance with the most eminent persons of an age so fruitful in *beaux Esprits*, inflamed his natural ardour to distinguish himself in the *belles Lettres*. He fancied that he was destined to be a great Poet, and the high compliments he received from one, who was really such, confirmed him in that error. Whether this doth not create some doubt of that sincerity and plain-dealing, on which Mr. POPE piqued himself so much, I leave to be determined by those, who understand the motives on which he acted. His noble friend had been equally lavish in his praises of Mr. HILL, and the grounds of Mr. POPE's quarrel with both, or rather, of their quarrel with him, were juſt the ſame. When he found it neceſſary to be more temperate in his commendations, this honeſt reſerve was called ill treatment. Among authors there is nothing ſo common as theſe effects of extravagant, or ill-placed approbation.

From Poetry to Muſic the paſſage was natural and eaſy. But from compoſing Dramas to be ſet, to the extracting oil from Beech-nuts, was a tranſition quite peculiar to ſuch a verſatile genius as Mr. HILL. The connexion betwixt the orcheſtra and the alembic it is difficult to diſcover.

To return to our account of RINALDO. In this Opera the famous NI-

NICOLINI fung. Its fuccefs was very great, and his engagements at Hanover the fubject of much concern with the lovers of Mufic. For when he could return to England, or whether he could at all, was yet very uncertain. His Playing was thought as extraordinary as his Mufic. One of the principal performers here ufed to fpeak of it with aftonifhment, as far tranfcending that of any perfon he had ever known, and as quite peculiar to himfelf. Another, who had affected to difbelieve the reports of his abilities before he came, was heard to fay, from a too great confidence in his own, " Let " him come! we'll Handle him, " I warrant ye!" There would be no excufe for recording fo poor a pun, if any words could be found, capable of conveying the

cha-

character of the speaker with equal force and clearness. But the moment he heard HANDEL on the organ, this great man in his own eye shrunk into nothing.

He had now been a full twelvemonth in England, and it was time for him to think of returning to Hanover. When he took leave of the Queen at her court, and expressed his sense of the favours conferred on him, her Majesty was pleased to add to them by large presents, and to intimate her desire of seeing him again. Not a little flattered with such marks of approbation from so illustrious a personage, he promised to return, the moment he could obtain permission from the Prince, in whose service he was retained.

Soon

Soon after his return to Hanover he made twelve chamber Duettos for the practice of the late Queen, then electoral Princess. The character of these is well known to the judges in Music. The words for them were written by the Abbate MAURO HORTENSIO, who had not disdained on other occasions to minister to the masters of harmony.

Besides these Duettos (a species of composition of which the Princess and court were particularly fond) he composed variety of other things for voices and instruments.

Towards the end of the year 1712, he obtained leave of the Elector to make a second visit to England, on condition that he engaged to return within a reasonable time.

It was not many months after his arrival at LONDON that the peace of Utrecht was brought to a conclusion. Each year of this memorable reign had been so crowded with heroic atchievements and grand events, that the poets and painters of our island seem to have sunk, as it were, under the load of matter, which had been heaped upon them. And had our musicians been thought equal to the task, a foreigner would hardly have been applied to for the song of triumph and thanksgiving, which was now wanted. The illustrious family which had taken HANDEL into its patronage, had not only been deeply concerned, but highly distinguished, in the
course

course of the war. The military talents, and personal bravery of its members had contributed to its prosperous issue. And not only the august house of Hanover, but most of the protestant Princes of the country to which he was indebted for his birth and education, had concurred in the reduction of that overgrown power, which long had menaced their religion and liberty. These circumstances produced that particular sort of interest and attachment, which, when joined to the dignity and importance of a subject, dispose an artist to the utmost exertion of his powers. No performance can be thoroughly excellent, unless it is wrought *con amore*, as the Italians express it. HANDEL, it must be owned, had all these advantages. And it is not too much, perhaps it is too little to fay, that the work was anfwerable to them. But let the grand Te Deum and Jubilate fpeak for themfelves! Our bufinefs is not to play the panegyrift, but the hiftorian.

The great character of the Operas which Handel had made in Italy and Germany, and the remembrance of Rinaldo joined with the poor proceedings at the Haymarket, made the nobility very defirous that he might again be employed in compofing for that theatre. To their applications her Majefty was pleafed to add the weight of her own authority; and, as a teftimony of her regard to his merit, fettled upon him a penfion for life of 200 *l. per Annum.*

This

This act of the royal bounty was the more extraordinary, as his foreign engagements were not unknown.

Of the several Operas which he made during this period some account will be given in another place. The time had again elapsed to which the leave he had obtained, could in reason be extended. But whether he was afraid of repassing the sea, or whether he had contracted an affection for the diet of the land he was in; so it was, that the promise he had given at his coming away, had somehow slipt out of his memory.

On the death of the Queen in 1714, his late Majesty came over. HANDEL, conscious how ill he had deserved at the hands of his gracious patron, now invited to the throne of thefe kingdoms by all the friends of our happy and free conftitution, did not dare to fhew himfelf at court. To account for his delay in returning to his office, was no eafy matter. To make an excufe for the non-performance of his promife, was impoffible. From this ugly fituation he was foon relieved by better luck than perhaps he deferved. It happened that his noble friend Baron Kilmanfeck was here. He, with fome others among the nobility, contrived a method for reinftating him in the favour of his Majefty; the clemency of whofe nature was foon experienced by greater perfons on a much more trying occafion.

The King was perfuaded to form a party on the water. HANDEL

was

was apprifed of the defign, and advifed to prepare fome Mufic for that occafion. It was performed and conducted by himfelf, unknown to his Majefty, whofe pleafure on hearing it was equal to his furprife. He was impatient to know whofe it was, and how this entertainment came to be provided without his knowledge. The Baron then produced the delinquent, and afked leave to prefent him to his Majefty, as one that was too confcious of his fault to attempt an excufe for it; but fincerely defirous to attone for the fame by all poffible demonftrations of duty, fubmiffion, and gratitude, could he but hope that his Majefty, in his great goodnefs, would be pleafed to accept them. This interceffion was accepted without any difficulty. HANDEL was reftored to favour, and his

Mufic

Music honoured with the highest expressions of the royal approbation. As a token of it, the King was pleased to add a pension for life of 200 *l.* a year to that which Queen Anne had before given him. Some years after, when he was employed to teach the young Princesses, another pension of the same value was added to the former by her late Majesty.

In the year 1715, he made the Opera of Amadige, as appears from the list annexed. I cannot find that he was employed in making any others between this time and the year 1720, excepting those of Teseo and Pastor Fido: for tho' they have no dates to inform us with certainty when they were composed, they are known to have been among his earliest productions

of

of this kind, and muſt have been performed in ſome part of the interval above-mentioned.

During the three firſt years of it, he was chiefly, if not conſtantly, at the Earl of BURLINGTON's. The character of this nobleman, as a ſcholar and virtuoſo, is univerſally known. As Mr. POPE was very intimate with his Lordſhip, it frequently happened that he and HANDEL were together at his table. After the latter had played ſome of the fineſt things he ever compoſed, Mr. POPE * declared,

---

* The Poet one day aſked his friend Dr. ARBUTHNOT, of whoſe knowledge in Muſic he had a high idea, What was his real opinion in regard to HANDEL as a Maſter of that Science? The Doctor immediately replied, "Conceive the higheſt that you can of his abilities, and they are much beyond any thing that you can conceive."

clared, that they gave him no fort of pleafure; that his ears were of that untoward make, and reprobate caft, as to receive his Mufic, which he was perfuaded was the beft that could be, with as much indifference as the airs of a common ballad. A perfon of his excellent underftanding, it is hard to fufpect of affectation. And yet it is as hard to conceive, how an ear fo perfectly attentive to all the delicacies of rhythm and poetical numbers, fhould be totally infenfible to the charms of mufical founds. An attentivenefs too, which was as difcernible in his manner of reading, as it is in his method of writing. But perhaps the extravagant and injudicious praifes, which the paffionate admirers of the Art are apt to beftow on fuch occafions, might provoke one of his fatyric turn to

exprefs

express himself more strongly than he would otherwise have done. Perhaps too, a Genius so fond of *exploring* characters, and so eminently skilled in *drawing* them, might think such an Artist as HANDEL a proper subject for experiments in this way. The greatest talents are often accompanied with the greatest weaknesses. But the Bard was much deceived if he imagined him weak enough to be mortified by a declaration, which, whether real or pretended, deserved not the least regard. HANDEL minded it just as much as POPE would have done a like assurance from *him* with respect to Poems, which all the world besides have agreed to admire.

The remaining two years he spent at CANNONS, a place which was

was then in all its glory, but remarkable for having much more of art than nature, and much more coſt than art. Of the Muſic he made for the Chapel there, ſome account will be given in another place. Whether HANDEL was *provided* as a mere implement of grandeur, or *choſen* from motives of a ſuperior kind, it is not for us to determine. This one may venture to aſſert, that the having ſuch a Compoſer, was an inſtance of *real* magnificence, ſuch as no private perſon, or ſubject; nay, ſuch as no prince or potentate on the earth could at that time pretend to.

During the laſt year of his reſidence at Cannons, a project was formed by the Nobility for erecting an academy at the Haymarket. The

The intention of this mufical Society, was to fecure to themfelves a conftant fupply of Operas to be compofed by HANDEL, and performed under his direction. For this end a fubfcription was fet on foot: and as his late Majefty was pleafed to let his name appear at the head of it, the Society was dignified with the title of the Royal Academy. The fum fubfcribed being very large, † it was intended to continue for fourteen years certain. But as yet it was in its embrio-ftate, being not fully formed till a year or two after.

HANDEL therefore, after he quitted his employment at Cannons, was advifed to go over to DRESDEN in queft of Singers. Here he engaged

† The KING fubfcribed 1000 *l.* and the Nobility 40,000 *l.*

gaged SENESINO and DURISTANTI, whom he brought over with him to ENGLAND.

At this time BUONONCINI and ATTILIO compofed for the Opera, and had a ftrong party in their favour. Great reafon they faw to be jealous of fuch a rival as HANDEL, and all the intereft they had was employed to decry his Mufic, and hinder him from coming to the Haymarket: but thefe attempts were defeated by the powerful affociation above-mentioned, at whofe defire he had juft been to Drefden for Singers.

In the year 1720, he obtained leave to perform his Opera of RADAMISTO. If perfons who are now living, and who were prefent at that performance may be credited,
the

the applause it received was almost as extravagant as his AGRIPPINA had excited: the crowds and tumults of the house at Venice were hardly equal to those at LONDON. In so splendid and fashionable an assembly of ladies (to the excellence of their taste we must impute it) there was no shadow of form, or ceremony, scarce indeed any appearance of order or regularity, politeness or decency. Many, who had forc'd their way into the house with an impetuosity but ill suited to their rank and sex, actually fainted through the excessive heat and closeness of it. Several gentlemen were turned back, who had offered forty shillings for a seat in the gallery, after having despaired of getting any in the pit or boxes.

But,

But, it may be thought, that the great excellence of SENESINO, both as to voice and action, might have a confiderable fhare in the wonderful impreffions made upon the audience. For, by virtue of great advantages in the reprefentation, many performances of little or no value, have not only paffed, but been well received.—To the ladies efpecially, the merits of SE-NESINO would be much more obvious, than thofe of HANDEL.— Perhaps they would. That *all* depended on the Compofer, I am as far from afferting, as I am from believing that any other perfon could have fhewn fuch a finger to equal advantage. Let any impartial and competent judge confider, whether it is likely that the whole mufical world could
have

have afforded a compofer befides himfelf, capable of furnifhing Senesino with fuch a fong, as that of Ombra Cara in the very Opera before us.

The great fuccefs of it matur'd the project before concerted for eftablifhing an academy. For it could not be effected at once, as a confiderable number of great perfons had been inftrumental in bringing over Buononcini and Attilio. And thefe foreigners they were the more unwilling to abandon, becaufe they really had abilities in their profeffion. Perhaps the contefts ran as high on both fides, as if the object of them had been much more important. Yet I cannot agree with fome, who think them of no importance, and treat them as ridiculous. Thofe who thought their honour engaged to fupport the old Compofers; who really preferred them to HANDEL; or fancied that it was a defect of humanity, or an act of injuftice to difcard them, not becaufe they were unfit for their office, but becaufe another foreigner was come, who was thought to be fitter; — had furely a right to intereft themfelves warmly in their defence, at a time when they were fo much in want of affiftance.

And thofe, on the other hand, might as reafonably join in oppofing them, who were firmly convinced of HANDEL's great fuperiority; and who thought it for the honour of the nation to inlift in its fervice the moft eminent artifts. The old ones, in their opinion, had no right to complain of any preference given to another, provided they were duly paid for the time they had been engaged. When disputes are carried on with any heat or violence, it is usually taken for granted, that both sides are in the wrong. But these qualities so disagreeable in their operation, are often salutary in their effects. Ill as things may seem to be managed with them, it is possible they might be managed worse without them. For these eager enquiries, and warm debates concerning what is fittest to be chosen and preferred, lead us to the knowledge of what is best and most perfect in the kind. By lighting up the flame of emulation in the breasts of contending artists, they contribute to the advancement of the art. Destroy these workings of passion, and there

there is an end of patriots, poets, and virtuosos.

Perhaps therefore the uses of quarrelling may compensate for all its inconveniences. But if not, the art of quarrelling, without losing one's temper, is, I fear, too difficult for even courts to teach or practise.—But I wander from my subject.

Such then was the state of things in the year 1720, at the time RA-DAMISTO was performed. The succeeding winter brought this musical disorder to its crisis. In order to terminate all matters in controversy, it was agreed to put them on this fair issue. The several parties concerned were to be jointly employed in making an Opera, in which each of them was to take a distinct act. And he, who by the general-suffrage, should be allowed to have given the best proofs of his abilities, was to be put into possession of the house. The proposal was accepted, whether from choice, or necessity, I cannot say. The event was answerable to the expectations of HANDEL's friends. His act was the last, and the superiority of it so very manifest, that there was not the least pretence for any further doubts or disputes. I should have mentioned, that as each made an overture, as well as an act, the affair seemed to be decided even by the overture with which HANDEL's began. The name of the Opera was MUZIO SCÆVOLA*.

The

---

* For further particulars of the overture in this Opera, see the note to page 44.

The academy being now firmly established, and HANDEL appointed Composer to it, all things went on prosperously for a course of between nine and ten years. And this may justly be called the period of musical glory, whether we consider the performances or the performers, most certainly not to be surpassed, if equalled, in any age or country. The names and dates of the Operas exhibited within this memorable interval, may be found in their regular series by turning to the catalogue. And some brief and general account of their character is given in the observations at the end of it.

The perfect authority which HANDEL maintained over the singers and the band, or rather the total

sub-

subjection in which he held them, was of more consequence than can well be imagined. It was the chief means of preserving that order and decorum, that union and tranquillity, which seldom are found to subsist for any long continuance in musical Societies. Indeed, all Societies, like the animal body, seem to carry in their very frame and frabric, the seeds of their own dissolution. This happens sooner or later, only as those are forwarded or retarded by different causes.

SENESINO, who, from his first appearance, had taken deep root, and had long been growing in the affections of those, whose right to dominion the most civilized nations have ever acknowledged, began to feel his strength and importance. He felt them so much, that
what

what he had hitherto regarded as legal government, now appeared to him in the light of downright tyranny Handel, perceiving that he was grown lefs tractable and obfequious, refolved to fubdue thefe Italian humours, not by lenitives, but fharp corrofives. To *manage* him he difdained; to controul him with a high-hand, he in vain attempted. The one was perfectly refractory; the other was equally outrageous. In fhort, matters had proceeded fo far, that there were no hopes of an accommodation. The merits of the quarrel I know nothing of. Whatever they were, the Nobility would not confent to his defign of parting with Senesino, and Handel was determined to have no farther concerns with him. Faustina and Cuzzoni, as if feized with the contagion of difcord,

discord, started questions of superiority, and urged their respective
claims to it with an eagerness and
acrimony, which occasioned a total dis-union betwixt them.

And thus the Academy, after it
had continued in the most flourish-
ing state for upwards of nine years,
was at once dissolved.

The late Laureat, who, now and
then, has some strokes of humour,
(for dulness too hath its lucid intervals) diverts himself much on the
subject of these musical frays. The
unlucky effects of them at the marriage of the late Duke of Parma,
he describes with that pert kind of
pleasantry, that native *gaillardise*
which attended him through life.
The fondness for Italian Singers,
he thinks unaccountable: the expence

pence and trouble they occasion, exorbitant and ridiculous. He calls them costly Canary-birds; and on their behaviour at the marriage solemnity just mentioned above, laments as follows, "What a pity it is, that these froward Misses and Masters of Music, had not been engaged to entertain the court of some King of Morocco, that could have known a good Opera from a bad one! With how much ease would such a Director have brought them to better order?"—But, had he known any thing of the true † spirit of HANDEL, he would not have wished them under better government.

† Having one day some words with CUZZONI on her refusing to sing *Falsa imagine* in OTTONE; Oh! Madame, (said he) je sçais bien que Vous êtes une veritable Diablesse: mais je Vous ferai sçavoir, moi, que je suis Beelzebub le *Chéf* des Diables. With this he took her up by the waist, and, if she made any more words,

ment. It is true they mutinied, and rebelled at laft. But the flaves of Afiatic and of African Monarchs, have often done as much.

He remained inflexible in his refolution to punifh SENESINO for refufing him that fubmiffion, which he had been ufed to receive, and which he thought he had a right to demand: but a little pliability would have faved him abundance of trouble. The vacancy made by the removal of fuch a Singer was not eafily fupplied. The umbrage which he had given to many of the Nobility, by his implacable refentments

words, fwore that he would fling her out of the window.

It is to be noted, that this was formerly one of the methods of executing criminals in fome parts of Germany; a procefs not unlike that of the Tarpeian rock, and probably derived from it.

ments against a person whose talents they so much admired, was likely to create him a dangerous opposition. For, tho' he continued at the Hay-market, yet, in the heat of these animosities, a great part of his audience would melt away. New Singers must be sought, and could not be had any nearer than Italy. The business of chusing, and engaging them, could not be dispatched by a deputy. And the party offended might improve the opportunity of his absence to his disadvantage.

In spite of all these discouragements, to Italy he went, as soon as he had settled an agreement with HEIDEGGAR to carry on Operas in conjunction with him. The agreement was for the short term of
three

three years, and so settled as to subsist only from year to year.

On his arrival at Rome, he received a very friendly and obliging letter of invitation from cardinal COLONNA, with a promise of a very fine picture of his Eminence. But, hearing that the Pretender was then at the Cardinal's, he prudently declined accepting both the invitation and the picture.

After a short stay in Italy, he returned with STRADA, BERNACHI, FABRI, BERTOLDI, and others. Being thus embarqued on a new bottom, he went on in conjunction with HEIDEGGER, but not with that even and prosperous gale which had wafted him so smoothly and pleasantly through the nine preceding years: for about the time of the

feparation at the Hay-market, oc--
cafioned by the difagreement be--
tween HANDEL and his Singers,
many of the Nobility raifed a new
fubfcription in order to carry on an--
other Opera at Lincoln's-inn-fields,
in which they could have Singers
and Compofers of their own chu--
fing. With this view they fent for
PORPORA, FARINELLI, and others.
The former was author of feveral
Cantatas which were much admi--
red, and gave great fatisfaction to
the perfons who employed him.
The latter charmed all hearers by
his exquifite voice, which he knew
how to manage to the beft advan--
tage. Tho' HANDEL bore up with
great fpirit and firmnefs againft
this oppofition, he foon felt the
effects of it; and yet, at the expi--
ration of the three years partnerfhip
with HEIDEGGER, he ventured to
continue

continue Operas at the Hay-market for one year on his own bottom. Finding this attempt no way likely to succeed, he left the Hay-market, and on the return of the adverse party to it, removed to the vacant theatre at Lincoln's-inn-fields. Here he continued but a little while; for he considered that the tide of opposition was now at its full heighth, and that to stem it, his own strength, superior as it was, might not be sufficient. The little taste he had already had of adversity, lessened that self-confidence which success is apt to inspire. He found that it was not the necessary consequence of great abilities, and that without prudence the greatest may be almost annihilated in the opinions of men. But it is a principal part of prudence, to command our temper on any trial we may chance to receive; a part of it which, to say the truth, he never practised or professed. This omission involved him in misfortunes, which taught him another part of prudence (if it must be called so) which he never ought to have practised, much less professed, that of consulting his interest at the expence of his art.

He now removed to Convent-garden, and entered into a partnership with RICH, the master of that house. HASSE and PORPORA were the Composers at the Hay-market. When the former was invited over, it is remarkable, that the first question he asked, was, whether HANDEL was dead. Being answered in the negative, he refused to come, from a persuasion, that where his countryman was (for they were both Saxons by birth) no other person of
the

the fame profeſſion was likely to make any figure. He could not believe that in a nation which had always been famous for fenfe and difcernment, the credit of fuch an artift as HANDEL could ever be impaired. However, this myſtery was explained to him in fuch a manner, and this explanation accompanied by fuch offers, that at length he got the better of his fcruples, and confented to be engaged. He is remarkable for his fine elevated air, with hardly fo much as the fhew of harmony to fupport it. And this may ferve not only for a character of HASSE in particular, but of the Italians in general, at the time we are fpeaking of. The oppofition in which they were engaged againſt HANDEL, made him look upon that merit in his antagoniſts with much indifference, and upon this defect with still more contempt. He carried his contempt so far, as to endeavour to be as unlike them as possible. He could have vanquished his opponents at their own weapons; but he had the sense to discover, that the offended and prejudiced side would never have acknowledged his victory however decisive; and that his new friends, for want of understanding the nature and use of such weapons, would not have discerned it however obvious. From hence he gradually fell into that too close and particular attachment to the harmony, which sometimes led him to neglect the melody, even where it ought most to be regarded, I mean in Vocal Music. A farther account of the causes and consequences of this omission, may be found in the observations on his works.

In the summer of the year 1733, he made a tour to OXFORD, where there was a public Act, at which he performed his Oratorio of ATHALIAH, composed for that solemnity. By this journey the damages he had suffered in his fortune were somewhat repaired, and his reputation more firmly established. The next winter his Opera of ARIANNA was performed at Convent-garden, while another of the same name, composed by PORPORA, was acted at the Hay-market. POLYPHEMO by the same person, and ARTAXERXES by HASSE, gained great applause there soon after. Though HANDEL had some good Singers, none of them could be compared to FARINELLI, who drew all the world to the Hay-market. And it soon appeared that the relish of the English for Music, was not strong enough to support two Operas at a time. There were but few persons of any other class, besides that of the Nobility, who had much knowledge of the Italian, any notion of such compositions, or consequently any real pleasure in hearing them. Those among the middling and lower orders, whom affectation or curiosity had drawn to the Theatre at his first setting out in conjunction with RICH, fell off by degrees. His expences in providing Singers, and in other preparations, had been very large; and his profits were no way proportionate to such charges. At the end of three or four years, instead of having acquired such an addition to his fortune, as from his care, industry, and abilities, he had reason to expect, he was obliged

ged to draw out of the funds almost all that he was worth, in order to answer the demands upon him. This upshot put an end for the present to all musical entertainments at Convent-garden, and almost put an end to the author of them. The violence of his passions made such a disaster operate the more terribly.

The observation that misfortunes rarely come single, was verified in HANDEL. His fortune was not more impaired, than his health and his understanding. His right-arm was become useless to him, from a stroke of the palsy; and how greatly his senses were disordered at intervals, for a long time, appeared from an hundred instances, which are better forgotten than recorded. The most violent deviations from reason,

reason, are usually seen when the strongest faculties happen to be thrown out of course.

In this melancholic state, it was in vain for him to think of any fresh projects for retrieving his affairs. His first concern was how to repair his constitution. But tho' he had the best advice, and tho' the necessity of following it was urged to him in the most friendly manner, it was with the utmost difficulty that he was prevailed on to do what was proper, when it was any way disagreeable. For this reason it was thought best for him to have recourse to the vapor-baths of Aix la Chapelle, over which he sat near three times as long as hath ever been the practice. Whoever knows any thing of the nature of those baths, will, from this instance,

form

form some idea of his surprising constitution. His sweats were profuse beyond what can well be imagined. His cure, from the manner as well as from the quickness, with which it was wrought, passed with the Nuns for a miracle. When, but a few hours from the time of his quitting the bath, they heard him at the organ in the principal church as well as convent, playing in a manner so much beyond any they had ever been used to, such a conclusion in such persons was natural enough. Tho' his business was so soon dispatched, and his cure judged to be thoroughly effected, he thought it prudent to continue at Aix about six weeks, which is the shortest period usually allotted for bad cases.

Soon after his return to London in 1736, his ALEXANDER's FEAST was performed at Convent-Garden, and was well received.

After much mifmanagement, and various mifunderftandings at the Hay-market, the glories of that theatre feemed quite extinct. Lord MIDDLESEX, defirous of feeing the Opera reftored to its former fplendor, undertook the direction of it, and applied to HANDEL, as the fitteft perfon to fupply it with compofitions. He made two Operas for his Lordfhip, FARAMONDO and ALESSANDRO SEVERO; the laft of which was a Pafticcio, and performed, as well as the other, in the year 1737. For thefe he received 1000*l*. Had he been difpofed to make any conceffions, his friends might eafily have effected a reconciliation between him and his opponents. All parties would in that cafe have been

glad

glad to have seen him again at the Hay-market; for at this time all the sources of Opera-music seem to have been drained to the very dregs. The sense of his abilities, the present exigency in which they were so much wanted, the recollection of his losses and sufferings; time itself, which as it consumes many valuable things, so it often happily wears out personal resentments:—In short, every thing seemed to concur, and nothing was wanting to insure his future prosperity, excepting a spirit which knew how to yield on proper occasions. From a single benefit made for him at the Haymarket in the year 1738, from which he is said to have received 1500 *l.* it is easy to guess what might have been done to recover his affairs. But he was so averse to subscription-engagements, that he resolved to be for the future on a quite different footing. No prospects of advantage could tempt him to court those by whom he thought he had been injured and oppressed. Full of these lofty sentiments, he returned to Convent-Garden, where he performed a few more Operas, the dates of which may be found in the catalogue. Finding that the taste of his audience was naturally averse to this species of composition, he now introduced another, more suited to the native gravity and solidity of the English, tho' borrowed from the *concert spirituel* of their volatile neighbours on the continent. ESTHER was made originally for the Duke of CHANDOIS, about a year after ACIS *and* GALATEA. After it had been performed at Cannons, it was played

at

at the Crown and Anchor; and this indeed is said to have first furnished the hint for bringing Oratorios on the stage. As the most remarkable characters, events, and occurrences contained in the holy scriptures, are intended to be represented in these solemn pieces, it is plainly of their nature to be acted, as well as sung, and accompanied. But the very sacredness and solemnity of the subjects treated, made even the setting them to Music appear to some persons little less than a prophanation. What strengthened this opinion was probably this, that most of the relations which are the subject matter of Operas are taken from prophane and fabulous history. And though Music was allowed to lend its assistance in places of worship; yet it seemed to be a dangerous innovation to allow it the further

pri-

privilege of canvassing in full form religious subjects in places of entertainment. It seemed to be forming a sort of alliance between things usually considered in a state of natural opposition, the church and theatre. In times when narrow notions were more in vogue, and when even men of sense were governed rather by appearances than by realities, Oratorios would not have been tolerated. In these happier days the influence of prejudice was not indeed quite strong enough to exclude these noble performances, yet it is even still strong, enough to spoil them. For are not the very same arguments which prevailed for admitting Oratorios sufficient to justify the acting them?

Would not action and gesticulation accommodated to the situation and

and sentiments, joined with dresses conformable to the characters represented, render the representations more expressive and perfect, and consequently the entertainment much more rational and improving*. Provided no improper characters were introduced, (a thing easy to be obviated) what other inconvenience could possibly result from the further allowance here contended for, it is hard to imagine. But this is spoken with perfect submission to the proper judges.

About

Racine's Esther and Athaliah set by Lulli, and performed at the convent of St. Cyr, by Order of Madame de Maintenon, had all the advantages of theatrical imitation. Indeed the best performance, if properly dramatic, without the helps of suitable action, and proper dresses, must needs lose a considerable part of that force and clearness, that life and spirit, which result from a full and perfect exhibition.

About the year 1729, or 1730, Esther and Deborah had been performed at the Hay-market with good fuccefs; with much better indeed than he met with at Convent-Garden, when he tried them there but a few years after. He feems not fufficiently to have confidered the rifques which he ran in this new undertaking. The diftance of this theatre from thofe parts of the town where the nobility chiefly refide; the relics of the oppofition not yet extinct, though fomewhat abated; a ftyle little fuited as yet to the apprehenfions of the generality;—thefe, and probably fome other caufes, may have concurred to render his attempt inaufpicious in its commencement. Too much accuftomed to difappointments to be eafily difpirited, he continued

thefe

these new entertainments, so excellently adapted to the season of the year in which they are exhibited, till the beginning of the year 1741. But at this time his affairs again carried so ill an aspect, that he found it necessary to try the event of another peregrination. He hoped to find that favour and encouragement in a distant capital, which London seemed to refuse him. For even his MESSIAH had met with a cold reception. Either the sense of musical excellence was become so weak, or the power of prejudice so strong, that all the efforts of his unparalleled genius and industry proved ineffectual.

DUBLIN has always been famous for the gaiety and splendor of its court, the opulence and spirit of its principal inhabitants, the valour of its military, and the genius of its learned men. Where fuch things were held in efteem he rightly reckoned, that he could not better pave the way to his fuccefs, than by fetting out with a ftriking inftance and public act of generofity and benevolence. The firft ftep that he made, was to perform his MESSIAH for the benefit of the cityprifon. Such a defign drew together not only all the lovers of Mufic, but all the friends of humanity. There was a peculiar propriety in this defign from the fubject of the Oratorio itfelf; and there was a peculiar grace in it from the fituation of HANDEL's affairs. They were brought into a better pofture by his journey to Dublin, where he ftaid between eight and nine months. The reception that he met with, at the fame time that it

fhewed

shewed the strong sense which the Irish had of his extraordinary merit, conveyed a kind of tacit reproach on all those on the other side of the water, who had enlisted in the opposition against him. Mr. POPE in the fourth book of the DUNCIAD has related this passage of his history. A poor phantom, which is made to represent the genius of the modern ITALIAN Opera, expresses her apprehensions, and gives her instructions to Dulness, already alarmed for her own safety. The lines are well known, but, for their strong characteristic imagery, deserve to be quoted in this place. They are as follows,

But soon, ah soon, rebellion will commence,
If Music meanly borrows aid from Sense:
Strong in new arms, lo! giant HANDEL stands,
Like bold BRIARIUS with his hundred hands;

To ſtir, to rouſe, to ſhake the ſoul he comes,
And Jove's own thunders follow Mars's drums.
Arreſt him, empreſs; or you ſleep no more —
She heard,—and drove him to the Hibernian ſhore.

At his return to London in 1741-2, the minds of moſt men were much more diſpoſed in his favour. He immediately recommenced his Oratorios at Convent-Garden. Sampson was the firſt he performed. And now (to uſe the expreſſive phraſe of Tacitus) *blandiebatur cœptis fortuna*; Fortune ſeemed rather to court and careſs, than to countenance and ſupport him. This return was the æra of his proſperity. Indeed, in the year 1743, he had ſome return of his paralytic diſorder; and the year after fell under the heavy diſpleaſure of a certain faſhionable lady. She

She exerted all her influence to fpirit up a new oppofition againſt him. But the world could not long be made to believe that her card-affemblies were fuch proper entertainments for Lent, as his Oratorios. It is needlefs to enlarge upon particulars which are eafily remembered, or to give a minute account of things generally known. It is fufficient juft to touch on the moſt remarkable. What is very much fo, his MESSIAH which had before been received with fo much indifference, became from this time the favourite Oratorio. As in the year 1741, it was applied to the relief of perfons expofed to all the miferies of perpetual confinement; it was afterwards confecrated to the fervice of the moft innocent, moft helplefs, and moſt diftreffed part of the human fpecies. The Foundling

ling Hofpital originally refted on the flender foundation of private benefactions. At a time when this inftitution was yet in its infancy; when all men feemed to be convinced of its utility; when nothing was at all problematical but the poffibility of fupporting it;—Handel formed the noble refolution to lend his affiftance, and perform his Messiah annually for its benefit. The fums raifed by each performance were very confiderable, and certainly of great confequence in fuch a crifis of affairs. But what was of much greater, was the magic of his name, and the univerfal character of his facred Drama. By thefe vaft numbers of the nobility and gentry were drawn to the hofpital; and many, who, at the firft, had been contented with barely approving the defign, were afterwards warmly

engaged

engaged in promoting it. In confequence of this refort, the attention of the nation was alfo drawn more forcibly to what was indeed the natural object of it. So that it may truly be affirmed, that one of the nobleft and moft extenfive charities that ever was planned by the wifdom, or projected by the piety of men, in fome degree owes its continuance, as well as profperity, to the patronage of HANDEL.

The very fuccefsful application of this wonderful production of his genius to fo beneficent a purpofe, reflected equal honour on the Artift and the Art.

He continued his Oratorios with uninterrupted fuccefs, and unrivalled glory, till within eight days of his death: the laft was performed on on the 6th of April, and he expired on Saturday the 14th of April 1759. He was buried the 20th by Dr. Pearce, Bishop of Rochester, in Westminster-abbey, where, by his own order, and at his own expence, a monument is to be erected to his memory.

In the year 1751, a gutta serena deprived him of his sight. This misfortune sunk him for a time into the deepest despondency. He could not rest until he had undergone some operations as fruitless as they were painful. Finding it no longer possible for him to manage alone, he sent to Mr. Smith to desire that he would play for him, and assist him in conducting the Oratorios.

His faculties remained in their full vigour almoſt to the hour of his diſſolution, as appeared from Songs and Choruſſes, and other Compoſitions, which from the date of them, may almoſt be conſidered as his parting words, his laſt accents! This muſt appear the more ſurpriſing, when it is remembered to how great a degree his mind was diſordered, at times, towards the latter part of his life.

His health had been declining apace for ſeveral months before his death. He was very ſenſible of its approach, and refuſed to be flattered by any hopes of a recovery. One circumſtance was very ominous, I mean the total loſs of appetite, which was come upon him, and which muſt prove more pernicious

cious to a perfon always habituated, as he had been, to an uncommon portion of food and nourifhment. Thofe who have blamed him for an exceffive indulgence in this loweft of gratifications, ought to have confidered, that the peculiarities of his conftitution were as great as thofe of his character. Luxury and intemperance are relative ideas, and depend on other circumftances befides thofe of quantity and quality. It would be as unreafonable to confine HANDEL to the fare and allowance of common men, as to expect that a London merchant fhould live like a Swifs mechanic. Not that I would abfolve him from *all* blame on this article. He certainly paid more attention to it, than is becoming in any man: but it is fome excufe, that Nature had given him fo vigorous a conftitution, fo

exquifite

exquisite a palate, and so craving an appetite; and that fortune enabled him to obey these calls, to satisfy these demands of Nature. They were really such. For besides the several circumstances just alledged, there is yet another in his favour; I mean his incessant and intense application to the studies of his profession. This rendered constant and large supplies of nourishment the more necessary to recruit his exhausted spirits. Had he hurt his health or his fortune by indulgences of this kind, they would have been vicious: as he did not, they were at most indecorous. As they have been so much the subject of conversation and pleasantry, to have taken no notice of them, might have looked like affectation. But it would be folly to enter into the particulars of this part

part of his history, and contrary to the design of the foregoing sheets, which is only "to give the Reader those parts of his † character, as a Man, that any way tend to open and explain his character as an Artist." So that the connection between this account of his life, and the following observations on his works, is closer than, at first sight, may be imagined. How far the materials

† It was thought better to leave the Reader to collect his character from the LIFE itself, than to attempt the drawing of it in form: a practice which has not succeeded over-much, even where it is most necessary; I mean in the writings of Historians. Truth hath seldom been so much as consulted in these studied representations. That constant and uniform opposition of the several parts, which, with much force and straining, are made to tally with each other, renders *most* characters only a more extended antithesis, and is scarce ever found really to exist in *any*. Yet often is this spurious brood of affectation and wit, palmed upon the world for the genuine offspring of education and nature.

materials for the former may be worth the digefting, can fairly be determined only by examining them in this view. How far they are well digefted, is another queftion, which every one will determine for himfelf, excepting the perfon employed in this attempt. But for his induftry in collecting them, fuch as they are, they would probably have been loft in the courfe of a few years. He has nothing to add, but his fincere wifhes, that every Artift, who is truly deferving in his profeffion, may meet with a perfon equally defirous of doing juftice to his memory.

F I N I S.

CATALOGUE

OF THE

WORKS

OF

George Frederic Handel.

L

I Think that the works of HANDEL may conveniently be distributed into three classes, *viz.*

1.
CHURCH-MUSIC.

2.
THEATRICAL MUSIC.

3.
CHAMBER-MUSIC.

And these again into ten inferior or lesser classes, *viz.*

1. ANTHEMS *and* TE DEUMS.
2. ORATORIOS.
3. OPERAS.
4. CONCERTOS, *for* Instruments.
5. SONATAS, *for two* Violins *and a* Bass.

6. Lessons, *for the* Harpsichord.
7. Chamber-Duettos.
8. Terzettos.
9. Cantatas *and* Pastoral Pieces.
10. Occasional, *or* Festal Pieces.

In the following catalogue there are several compositions, *viz.* Allegro ed il Penseroso, Triumph *of* Time *and* Truth, &c. which are placed among the Oratorios, because they were performed as such, but do not properly belong to that species. Indeed they cannot be said to fall under any of the classes above described. However they are not of consequence enough to form a distinct one among the lesser, any more than the Water-music among the larger.

As

As to the TRIUMPH *of* TIME *and* TRUTH, great part of the Mufic is the fame with that of IL TRIONFO DEL TEMPO, made at Rome many years before, revived in 1757, and performed only once at the Haymarket [in Italian] about the time the Oratorios firft began.

A great quantity of Mufic, not mentioned in the Catalogue, was made in Italy and Germany. How much of it is yet in being, is not known. Two chefts-full were left at HAMBURGH, befides fome at HANOVER, and fome at HALL.

THEATRICAL MUSIC.

OPERAS.

ALMERIA, made and performed at
    Hamburgh.

FLORINDA, Hamburgh.

NERONE, ditto.

RODERIGO, Florence.

AGRIPPINA, Venice.

IL TRIONFO DEL TEMPO, Rome. [Serenata.]

ACIGE E GALATEA, Naples. [Serenata.]

RINALDO, London, 1710.

TESEO, ditto.

AMADIGE, ditto, 1715.

PASTOR FIDO, ditto.

RADAMISTO, ditto. 1720.

MUZIO SCÆVOLA, ditto, 23 March, 1721.

OTTONE, ditto, 10 August, 1722.

FLORIDANTE, ditto. ——— 1723.

FLAVIO, ditto.— 7 May, 1723.

JULIO CÆSARE, ditto—- 1723.

TAMERLANE, ditto, 23 July 1724.

RODELINDA, ditto, 20 Jan. 1725.

SCIPIONE, ditto, 2 March 1726.

ALESSANDRO, ditto; 11 April 1726.

RICARDO,

Ricardo, London, 16 May 1727.
Ammeto, ditto, 16 May 1727.
Siroe, ditto, 5 February 1728.
Ptolomeo, ditto, 19 April 1728.
Lotario, ditto, 16 Nov. 1729.
Partenope, ditto, 12 Feb. 1730.
Poro, ditto, 26 January, 1731.
Sosarme, ditto, 4 February 1732.
Orlando, ditto, 20 Nov. 1732.
Ezio, ditto, 1733.
Arianna, ditto, 5 October 1733.
Ariodante, ditto, 24 Oct. 1734.
Alcina, ditto, 8 April 1735.
*Atalanta, ditto, 20 April 1736.
Giustino, ditto, 7 Septemb. 1736.
Arminio, ditto, 30 Octob. 1736.
Berenice, ditto, 18 Jan. 1737.
Faramondo, ditto, 24 Dec. 1737.
Alessandro Severo, ditto. [Pasticcio.]
Serse, ditto, 6 February 1738.

* Performed at the Princess of Orange's wedding.

* Imeneo, ditto, 10 Oct. 1740.
Diedamia, London, 20 Oct. 1740.

Oratorios.

Deborah, 21 Feb. 1733.
Esther.
Athaliah, 7 June, 1733.
Alexander's Feast, 17 Jan. 1736.
Israel *in* Egypt, 11 Oct. 1738.
Allegro ed il Penseroso, 1739.
Saul, 1740.
Messiah, 12 April, 1741.
Sampson, 12 Oct. 1742.
† Semele, 4 July, 1743.
Susannah, 9 August, 1743.
Belshazzar.
Hercules, 17 August 1744.

Occa-

---

* Performed on occasion of his late Royal Highness the Prince of Wales's wedding.

† An English Opera, but called an Oratorio, and performed as such at Covent-Garden. The words of it by Congreve.

(153)

† OCCASIONAL ORATORIO, 1745.
JUDAS MACCHABÆUS, 11 Aug. 1746.
JOSEPH, 1746.
ALEXANDER BALUS, 30 June 1747.
JOSHUA, 18 Aug. 1747.
SOLOMON, 13 June 1748.
THEODORA, 18 July 1749.
JEPTHA, 20 Aug. 1751.
TRIUMPH *of* TIME *and* TRUTH.

SERENATAS.

IL TRIONFO DEL TEMPO, Rome.
ACIGE e GALATEA, Naples.
*ACIS *and* GALATEA, for the Duke of Chandois, about the year 1721.
PARNASSO IN FESTA, [an Italian entertainment, sung at the Haymarket.]
CHOICE OF HERCULES.

---

† Performed on occasion of the victory gained at Culloden, by his Royal Highness the DUKE OF CUMBERLAND.

* The words of this piece wrote by Mr. GAY.

Church-Music.

A grand Te Deum and Jubilate for the peace of Utrecht, 1713.

Four Coronation Anthems, 1727.

Several Anthems made for the Duke of Chandois between 1717, and 1720.

Several more; as a Funeral Service for her late Majesty Queen Caroline; in all about twenty-three.

Three more Te Deums; one of which was on the occasion of the victory at Dettingen.

Chamber-Music.

Cantatas, [the greatest part made at Hanover, and other places abroad; in all about 200.

Chamber-Duettos, [twelve made at Hanover, and two after he came to England.]

Serenatas,

Serenatas, [moſt of them made a-
broad, and ſome few at his firſt
coming to England, one of which
was for Queen ANNE, and performed at St. James's, but afterwards loſt.]

INSTRUMENTAL-MUSIC.

Muſic for the Water.
Concertos for different Inſtruments.
Sonatas for two Violins and a Baſs.
Harpſichord-Leſſons.
Twelve grand Concertos.
Twelve ditto for the Organ.

OBSERVATIONS

ON THE

WORKS

OF

George Frederic Handel.

BEFORE we enter on the examination of Handel's works, it is neceſſary to ſettle the meaning of ſome words, which, on other ſubjects have been uſed with no great care, but never perhaps with ſo little as when they have been applied to Muſic. It is of conſequence to underſtand them well: for, whether we would explain the grounds, or diſtinguiſh the kinds, or eſtimate the degrees of muſical excellence, recourſe muſt ſtill be had to theſe expreſſions. A clear notion of the ſubject to which they are applied, will direct us to their true meaning.

Muſic

Music is founded on established rules and principles. There are certain relations and proportions which subsist between sounds, and certain effects, which are constantly and regularly † produced by their different union, arrangement, and combination. The rules are derived from experience and observation, which inform us what particular system or disposition of sounds will produce the most pleasing effects. A clear comprehension of those rules, and the ability to apply them, are called *knowledge:* and

---

† It is almost needless to make exceptions with regard to those who dislike Music, or who never attend to its effects. For (as the Abbé Du Bos says) Il est des hommes tellement insensibles à la Musique, & dont l'oreille (pour me servir de cette expression) est tellement eloignée du cœur, que les chants les plus naturels ne les touchent pas.

and this alone, without any great
ſhare either of *invention* or *taſte*,
may make a tolerable Compoſer.
But either of theſe joined with it,
forms a maſter.

The maſters may be diſtinguiſhed
into two claſſes, as their principal
merit conſiſts in *invention* or *taſte*.
The former of theſe ſeems to con-
ſiſt in the quick inveſtigation of
new, or hitherto-unperceived relations; in the combining theſe relations after an unuſual manner, or
according to a different order; and
in the happy application of them
to particular ſubjects, eſpecially to
ſuch as are of an important or in-
tereſting nature.

Thoſe who have an *inventive*
genius will depart from the common rules, and pleaſe us the more

by such deviations. These must of course be considered as bold strokes, or daring flights of fancy. Such passages are not founded on rules, but are themselves the foundation of new rules.

On the other hand, they who have *taste*, or a nice discernment of the minuter circumstances that please, will polish and improve the inventions of others. These will adhere strictly to rules, and even make them more strict.

Hence we may discern the reason why great *invention* and perfect *taste* are seldom, or never united, altho' either the one or the other may *meet* with *knowledge*.

Hence too we may conclude, that the merit of HANDEL's Music
will

will be least discerned by the lovers of elegance and correctness. They are shocked with every defect of this sort, while their very character hinders them from entering into those excellencies of a higher nature, in which he so much surpasses all other Musicians: excellencies, which are hardly consistent with a constant regard to those minuter circumstances, on which beauty depends. As *taste* implies a natural sensibility, and an habitual attention to these very circumstances, all neglects of them fall under its jurisdiction. But as this faculty is of a tender and timid nature, it is apt to consider those bolder strokes and rougher dashes which genius delights in, either as coarse, or as extravagant. However, when it attempts to chastise or correct such passages, it
mistakes

miftakes its province. Art is *here* not only ufelefs, but dangerous. It may eafily deftroy originality, tho' it cannot create elegance; which if it *could* be had, would be ill purchafed at the expence of the other. For the generality of mankind have not enough of delicacy to be much affected with minute inftances of beauty; but yet are fo formed, as to be tranfported with every the leaft mark of grandeur and fublimity.

What gives me the fuller affurance in the truth of thefe principles, is their agreement with the following obfervations, which a Gentleman, who is a perfect mafter of the fubject, was fo good as to communicate to me. The obfervations are as follows:

" As party and prejudice have been carried pretty high, on the one side in favour of Handel, and on the other in favour of the Italians, I shall endeavour to consider this affair with the impartiality it requires, and settle, to the best of my judgment, the merits on both sides.

The taste in Music both of the Germans and the Italians, is suited to the different characters of the two nations. That of the first is rough and martial; and their Music consists of strong effects produced, without much delicacy, by the rattle of a number of instruments. The Italians, from their strong and lively feelings, have endeavoured in their Music to express all the agitations of the soul, from the most

delicate

delicate senfations of love, to the moft violent effects of hatred and defpair; and this in a great degree by the modulation of a fingle part.

Handel formed his tafte upon that of his countrymen, but by the greatnefs and fublimity of his genius, he has worked up fuch effects as are aftonifhing. Some of the beft Italian mafters, by the delicacy of their modulation, have fo deeply entered into all the different fenfations of the human heart, that they may almoft be faid to have the paffions of mankind at their command; at leaft of that part of mankind, whofe lively feelings are fomewhat raifed to a pitch with their own.

When we confider two kinds of Mufic fo very different in character, as that of HANDEL, and that of the best Italians, and both carried to so great a degree of perfection, we cannot be surprised at seeing such warm advocates for each. HANDEL's Music must be allowed to have had some advantages over theirs, independent of its real merit. The fulness, strength, and spirit of his Music, is wonderfully well suited to the common sensations of mankind, which must be roused a little † roughly, and are not of a cast to be easily worked upon

---

† It is only HANDEL's *general* character that is here opposed to that of the Italians. For though the cast of his mind was *more* towards the great and sublime than any *other* style, yet he sometimes excels the Italians themselves even in the passionate and pathetic. This appears from particular instances, which we shall have occasion to cite presently; and from others which might be cited. That these have been overlooked, is probably owing to the many instances of a contrary kind in his Oratories and elsewhere.

upon by delicacies. Thus he takes in all the unprejudiced part of mankind. For in his fublime ftrokes, of which he has many, he acts as powerfully upon the moft Knowing, as upon the Ignorant. Another advantage which he has over the Italians, is owing to themfelves. The quantity of bad Mufic we have had from Italy, prejudices many againft the good. And here it may not be amifs to fay fomething of the prefent ftate of the Italian Mufic.

The old Mufic, fuch as it was in the time of PALESTRINO, and thofe excellent Compofers in the Church ftyle, was performed by a number of voices: the harmony was full and varied; and the effects were produced by the able management of their fugues and
imita-

imitations through all the parts. This required great skill in Music, as well as genius: so that at that time no man could set up for a Composer, without a very profound knowledge of the rules of composition. It happened, as it naturally must when the study of Music engages men of great abilities, both as to genius and knowledge, that improvements were constantly arising from one quarter or another. By this means the art of modulating a single voice, so as to express the various passions and affections, was every day gaining ground, till VINCI and PERGOLESI carried it in some of their Songs to the highest pitch we can as yet have any idea of. With this exquisite expression in the voice, they have shewn equal skill in the management of the instruments that accompany it. For their

instru-

instrumental parts are so judiciously contrived, that they are constantly adding new beauties to the Song-part without ever overwhelming it.

I cannot but lament that the Song-music which we have from Italy, has been dwindling ever since their time. And from the present situation of things, I think there is but little reason to hope that it will rise again. The Italian Composers have two things strongly against them, and which I conceive to be the cause of all the trifling, frothy Music we have at this time. The one is, the little time they have for composing. For as soon as any rising genius has given some striking proof of his abilities, the Managers of almost every Opera in Italy, want to engage him to compose for them.

The

The young fellow thinks his reputation is eftablifhed, and endeavours to make the moft of it, by undertaking to compofe as much as it is poffible to do in the time. This obliges him to write down any thing that firft prefents itfelf: and thus his Opera is chiefly made up of old worn-out paffages haftily put together, without any new turn of expreffion, or harmony. Almoft every Compofer of genius in Italy, is an inftance of this. But the moft ftriking inftance I know is JOMELLI, who has in fome things fhewn himfelf to be equal to any Compofer that has gone before him, while in many others he does not appear even above the common rank. The other difficulty the Italian Opera-compofers have to ftruggle with, is the undue influence of the Singers over them. A
good

good Singer (which is equally applicable to both the fexes) feldom fails to make fuch a party in his favour, as it would not be prudent in the Compofer to difoblige. This in fome degree puts him under the Singer's direction in relation to his own Songs; which is in fact the being directed in his compofitions by a perfon that knows very little of Mufic, and that wants to fhine by playing all the tricks he has been able either to invent or to learn.

This being the prefent fituation of the Italian Compofers, it is not furprifing that their compofitions fhould be fo thin and flimfy. For it is hardly to be expected, that a Compofer will be at the pains to do all he can, when the low price he is to have for his Opera, will hardly find him bread, if he has fpent
much

much time upon it; and when he may rifque both bread and reputation by difpleafing a favourite Singer.

From all that has been faid, I would conclude, that both thofe who indifcriminately condemn HANDEL's compofitions, and thofe who in like manner condemn the Italian Mufic, are equally to blame as prejudiced or ignorant deciders. And I would recommend it to all true lovers of Mufic, to examine with candor, and I may even add, with fome degree of reverence, the compofitions of men, whofe great abilities in their profeffion do honour to human nature. I think it is highly probable, that whatever delicacies appear in HANDEL's Mufic, are owing to his journey into Italy; and likewife that the Italians

lians are much indebted to him for their management of the inftrumental parts that accompany the voice; in which indeed fome few of them have fucceeded admirably well. And as fome proof of HANDEL's influence in Italy, it is, I believe, an undoubted fact, that French-horns were never ufed there as an accompaniment to the voice, till HANDEL introduced them.

But however well fome of the Italians may have fucceeded in the management of the inftrumental parts in their Song-mufic, there is one point in which HANDEL ftands alone, and in which he may poffibly never be equalled; I mean in the inftrumental parts of his Choruffes, and full Church-mufic. In thefe he has given innumerable inftances of an unbounded genius.

In

In short, there is such a sublimity in many of the effects he has work'd up by the combination of instruments and voices, that they seem to be rather the effect of inspiraration, than of knowledge in Music."

But in order to make a right judgment of his abilities in Music, attention must constantly be had to its two different species, *viz.* the instrumental and vocal.

The excellence of the former consists in the strength and fulness of its † harmony: that of the latter

---

† This is to be understood with some limitation. For it is not meant that the excellence of Instrumental Music consists *altogether* in the strength and fulness of its harmony; but only that this is the perfection of it as contradistinguished from the Vocal. The Concertos of
TARTINI,

latter in the delicacy and propriety of its melody.

Now that fulnefs of harmony, which is effential to the one, may in fome cafes hurt, if it doth not deftroy, the perfection of the other. Rousseau has developed this matter wonderfully well in his *Lettre fur la Mufique Françoife*. And it is in this point that I think Handel is fometimes faulty, and the beft Italian mafters almoft conftantly right, although I do not carry my idea

Tartini, and of fome other firft-rate Compofers for inftruments, are ftrong proofs that the excellence of Inftrumental Mufic fhould not be confined to harmony alone. For the merit of thofe pieces confifts ftill more in the high and uncommon delicacy of the melody, than in the harmony, though excellent in its kind, and incomparably well contrived for the fetting off and ftrengthening the expreffion of the principal part.

idea of their perfection quite so far as Rousseau does.

As Operas and Oratorios plainly belong to the vocal class, the Recitative and Air must always be considered as the principal parts in such performances. Yet in some of Handel's, the Symphonies and Accompaniments, instead of shewing those parts to advantage, have absorbed them, as it were, in their own superior splendor. His uncommon strength in the instrumental way, which it was natural for him to be fond of displaying, may have been one reason for his falling into this fault. Another perhaps was the badness of some of his Singers; for there never was an Opera in which all of them were good. A judicious Composer will always take care that the worst ſhall have little to do. But unleſs the inſtruments by their predominant harmony, fill up the vacuities occaſioned by the abſence, or thinneſs of the vocal parts, the attention of the audience muſt neceſſarily languiſh: an inconvenience evidently greater than that of violating the rules of propriety, by giving to the inſtruments more ſtreſs than the ſubject will warrant.

It may alſo be added, that in ſo long a performance as that of an Opera, there muſt be many Airs in different ſtyles, and on different ſubjects. The fineſt modulations, continued too long, or repeated too often, would flatten upon the ear. Here again recourſe muſt be had to the inſtruments, which, by a little over-acting their part, gain attention to thoſe Songs of a lower claſs,
which

which serve to set off and recommend the others. So that we must not wonder, if in HANDEL's old Operas we meet with some * Songs, which, from the fulness of the parts, appear to be almost Concertos.

But how shall we excuse for those instances of coarseness and indelicacy which occur so frequently in the Airs of his Oratorios? For as the melody is a fundamental and essential part in vocal Music, it should seem that nothing can attone for the neglect of it. The best Painter would be blamed,

should

---

* Yet in many others all the parts are so nicely adjusted, and so well sustained, that the several instruments in his Orchestra, resemble the several personages in a fine piece of history-painting, all engaged and interested in the same subject, and all concurring, in their different situations, to the furtherance and execution of the principal design.

should he draw off the attention too much from the principal figure in his piece, however perfect, by the very high and exquisite finishing of some inferior object: but much more would he deserve to be blamed, if he left that figure the least finished, which all the rules of his art required to be the most so. Now in Music, though there may sometimes be occasion, as we have seen, for giving the instruments the ascendancy over the voices; yet never should the Song-parts be unmeaning or inexpressive, much less coarse or ordinary.

To speak the plain truth, Handel was not so excellent in Air, where there is no strong character to mark, or passion to express. He had not the art, for which the Italians have ever been remarkable,

the

the art of trifling with grace and delicacy. His turn was for greater things, in expressing which it is hard to say, whether he excelled most in his Air, or in his Harmony. This may be proved even from his Oratorios, where he has failed the most * and the oftenest. But in his old Operas there are numberless instances of his abilities in the vocal way, such as it would be difficult to parallel out of the greatest Masters, whose whole excellence lay in that particular species. I will only

* Some allowances must be made for the disadvantages he was under from the Audience, the Singers, and the Language, all of them changed for the worse.

A gentleman whom he had desired to look over JUDAS MACCHABÆUS, having declared his opinion of it; Well, (said HANDEL) to be sure you have picked out the best Songs, but you take no notice of that which is to get me all the money; meaning the worst in the whole Oratorio.

only refer the Reader to a few Songs in different styles, *viz.*

Un disprezzato affetto, }
     &   } in OTTONE.
* Affanni del pensier, }
Ombra cara, in RADAMISTO.
Men fedele, }
   &   } in ALESSANDRO.
Il mio cor, }

Here too he will see, that tho', in two of the Songs above-cited, there is great employment for the instruments; and though in all of them the parts which they have to execute, are exceedingly fine; yet they are so contrived, as not to eclipse

---

* An eminent Master, who was not on good terms with HANDEL, often declared the opinion he had of his abilities in very strong expressions. That great Bear (said he) was certainly inspired when he made this Song. He might have said the same with full as much justice of that which I have coupled with it.

eclipse the air or melody. At the same time that they relieve the ear by the beauty and variety of their accords, they † assist the voice in expressing the particular action, passion,

† After all, the vocal species is not more indebted to the instrumental, than this is to the other. Many instances might be produced to confirm this assertion, from the compositions of different Masters. But TARTINI's Music may almost be considered as one continued instance of it. All his melody is so truly vocal in its style and character, that those parts of it which do not exceed the compass and powers of a voice, one would almost imagine were intended to be sung. His most difficult passages bear the same character, which was very apparent, when they were executed by himself: and all the Italians were so strongly sensible of this, that in speaking of his manner of playing, they often made use of the following expression, *non suona, canta su'l violino.* The reason why the compositions of this great Master are admired by so few people in Egland, is that the Performers of them neither enter into the true character of the Music, nor play it according to the intention of its author. The more any piece

passion, or sentiment intended to be represented.

And here I may just take notice, that the proper place for most musical imitations, is in the Symphonies and Accompaniments. There are indeed some few sounds, which Nature herself employs to express the stronger emotions of the human heart, which the voice may imitate. But it is common for the Masters not only to forget the nature and * extent of this imitative power in

piece of Music is delicate and expressive, the more insipid and disagreeable must it appear under a coarse and unmeaning execution. Just as the most delicate strokes of humour in comedy, and the most affecting turns of passion in tragedy, will suffer infinitely more from being improperly read, than a common paragraph in a news-paper.

* See Mr. HARRIS's three treatises, in which this point is discussed with great judgment and accuracy.

in Music, but also to mistake the subject on which to employ it. A too close attachmment to some particular words in a sentence, hath often misled them from the general meaning of it. HANDEL himself, from his imperfect acquaintance with the English language, has sometimes fallen into these mistakes. A Composer ought never to pay this attention to single words, excepting they have an uncommon energy, and contain some passion or sentiment. To do HANDEL justice, he is generally great and masterly, where the language and poetry are well adapted to his purpose. The English tongue abounds with monosyllables and consonants. Tho' these cannot always be avoided, yet the writers of musical dramas should always pick out such as are the least harsh and disagreeable

able to the ear. The fame regard muſt be had to the ſentiments, as to the language. The more ſimple and natural they are, the more eaſily will Muſic expreſs them. There was a time (ſays Mr. ADDISON) when it was laid down as a maxim, that nothing was capable of being well ſet to Muſic, that was not nonſenſe. This ſatyr is equally juſt and beautiful. But tho' the ſenſe of ſuch productions cannot be too ſtrong, the poetry of them may be too fine. If it abounds with noble images, and high wrought deſcriptions, and contains little of character, ſentiment, or paſſion, the beſt Compoſer will have no opportunity of exerting his talents. Where there is nothing capable of being expreſſed, all he can do is to entertain his audience with mere ornamental paſſages

passages of his own invention. But graces and flourishes must rise from the subject of the composition in which they are employed, just as flowers and festoons from the design of the building. It is from their relation to the whole, that these minuter parts derive their value.

To return to our examination of HANDEL's works. In his Chorusses he is without a rival. That easy, natural melody, and fine flowing air, which runs through them, is almost as wonderful a peculiarity, as that perfect fulness and variety, amid which there seems however to be no part but what figures, and no note that could be spared.

His Anthems are choral throughout, and so excellent in their kind, that

that it would be difficult to conceive any thing of human production that is more fo. Thofe which he made for the Duke of Chandois's chapel are the leaft known, but far from being among the leaft excellent. It is true that in the admirable epiftle addreffed to Lord Burlington, the two following lines, viz.

" Light quirks of mufic, broken and uneven,
Make the foul dance upon a jig to heaven;"

which are meant to expofe the falfe tafte of fuch Mufic, as is either foreign to the fubject, or improper for the occafion, may appear to be levelled at HANDEL, as he was employed in compofing for the chapel of the nobleman, whofe miftaken notions of magnificence were fuppofed to be pointed at by more circumftances than one in the
lines

lines immediately preceding those I have quoted. But there are many reasons, which make it utterly improbable that any Music of HANDEL's is here intended. For though Mr. POPE was no judge himself of any productions on this subject, yet he had many friends who well understood them; and none indeed better than the very lord, to whom his epistle is addressed. Besides, the opinion which he actually entertained of HANDEL's abilities, may be gathered from those fine lines upon him, which are quoted, in his life, from the 4th book of the DUNCIAD. It is however no way improbable that the same chapel might have furnished instances of the egregious impropriety here ridiculed, after HANDEL ceased to compose for it. But whether it did or not, it was the Poet's business

ness to go through the several instances of a perverted taste, in which the scene he made choice of abounded perhaps more than any other.

The reader will excuse this digression, as it seemed necessary to guard against mistakes not less injurious to the judgment of Pope on the one hand, than to the honour of Handel on the other.

As his Oratorios are all, or most of them, on scripture-subjects, so the Chorusses in them are quite in the church-style; and it may be said without extravagance, that the sublime strokes they abound with, look more like the effects of illumination, than of mere natural genius. Out of a multitude of examples which might be produced,
I will

I will only remind the reader of the few following in the single Oratorio of MESSIAH, *viz.*

For unto us a child is born, &c.
Lift up your heads, O ye gates, &c.
Hallelujah, for the Lord God omnipotent reigneth, &c.

After these vast efforts of genius, we find him rising still higher in the three * concluding Chorusses, each of which surpasses the preceding, till in the winding up of the Amen, the ear is fill'd with such a glow of harmony, as leaves the mind in a kind of heavenly extasy.

There are indeed but few persons sufficiently versed in Music,

---

* Beginning with, " Worthy is the lamb that was slain."

to perceive either the particular propriety and juftnefs, or the general union and confent, of all the parts in thefe complicated pieces. However, it is very remarkable that fome perfons, on whom the fineft modulations would have little or no effect, have been greatly ftruck with HANDEL's Choruffes. This is probably owing to that grandeur of conception, which predominates in them; and which, as coming purely from Nature, is the more ftrongly, and the more generally felt.

It is true, that, in the wonderful performance above-mentioned, there are great inequalities, as in moft of HANDEL's: but whoever fhould examine it throughout, muft confider him as a down-right prodigy. I ufe this expreffion becaufe
there

there are no words capable of conveying an idea of his character, unless indeed I was to repeat those which Longinus has employed in his description of Demosthenes, every part of which is so perfectly applicable to Handel, that one would almost be persuaded it was intended for him †.

His excellence in another branch of vocal Music, *viz.* the Recitative, might easily be shewn either from his old Operas, or from the single Oratorio above-mentioned. For a specimen, the following passages will be sufficient:

Comfort ye, comfort ye, my people, saith your God,   Messiah.

---

† See the conclusion of Longinus's 33d Section.

Alma del gran Pompeo,
           Julio Cæsare.

To which we may add, that grand scene of the death of Bajazet in Tamerlane.

Without attempting to explain the causes of that forcible expression, and overpowering pathos, which breathe in these, and many other passages of his Recitative, I will only alledge these effects of Music, to shew that its true use, and greatest value, is to heighten the natural impressions of religion and humanity.

The Duettos and Terzettos were made at different times. Those which he made abroad having never been printed, are in very few hands, and but little known. As they are of a character somewhat different from his latter compositions of the same kind, and in some respects superior to them, they deserve particular notice. They were composed in the vigour of his faculties, not for the theatre, but for the closet. Nothing was to be sacrificed to the rude, undiscerning ear of the multitude; nor were invention and harmony to be given up for the poor purchase of an *encore*. The author had only himself to please, or scholars formed by himself: and let any one judge whether his composition was not likely to be the better for such circumstances. Indeed, as might well be expected, we find these admirable productions free from such marks of haste and negligence, as are seen, and should in all reason be excused, in the works of length, which he has since composed. When we complain of these productions as frequently defective with regard to taste and delicacy, we should do well to recollect how little of either belongs to that tribunal, before which their merits were to be decided. But to resume our examination of the Duettos. It is as hard to characterize these, as the other parts of HANDEL's works. Though they may be said to comprehend most styles, yet the manly and the nervous prevail upon the whole. Indeed, in some of them there is a sweetness and delicacy of modulation not inferior to that of the amiable STEFFANI; as in many there is a spirit and majesty to which he appears to have been a stranger.

It was not to be diffembled that the manly caft of HANDEL's mind often led him into a kind of melody ill fuited to the voice; that he was apt to depart from the ftyle which the fpecies of compofition demanded, and run into paffages purely inftrumental. Yet fo admirable is the contrivance, and fo beautiful the modulation in fome of thefe pieces, where this deviation is moft confpicuous; that the beft judge of Mufic, who examines them as a critic, will hardly have the heart to execute his office; and, while the laws of it compel him to arraign the fault, will almoft be forry to fee it corrected. That all this may not appear to be faid at random, let us enter a little into the particulars.

The Duetto beginning, " *Ammirarvi io fono intento,*" is a

beau-

beautiful example of a style truly vocal, and much resembling that of STEFFANI.

That beginning, "*Conservate*," is another instance of the same kind. The first movement of " *Sono liete*," is another; but the last movement of the same is instrumental. Of this we have, in a manner, the author's acknowledgment; for he introduced it afterwards, with some alteration, into the Overture of JUDAS MACCHABÆUS.

As examples of a spirited and beautiful manner unknown to the calm and easy STEFFANI, I shall only mention, among many others, " *Che vai pensando*," and " *Tacete*."

Among the Trios " *Quando non bò più core*," is an instance of the
instru-

instrumental style, carried so far, as to render the performance of it extremely difficult.

In some parts of these pieces, but more particularly in the Terzettos, it is curious to observe those vast conceptions of the choral kind, pent up within the narrow limits of two or three parts; and struggling as it were, for that enlargement, which has since permitted them to take their full sweep in the wide, and almost unbounded province of *Chorus*. To shew that this observation is not chimerical, it need only be recollected that one of the finest Chorusses in the ALLEGRO, and that very artificial one with which ALEXANDER's FEAST concludes, were made out of two of these Trios.

Though the Duettos and Trios in his Operas and Oratorios are not in general so chaste, or of so learned a cast, as those of which we have just been speaking, yet the musical reader will easily call to mind several of distinguished beauty. Such are the famous Trio in Acis and Galatea;— the Duetto, *" O death, where is thy sting,"* in Messiah; — *" From this dread scene,"* in Judas Macchabæus;— and *" Io t'abbraccio,"* in Rodelinda.

The only Serenata (properly so called) which he made here, was Acis and Galatea; and it is one of the most equal and perfect of all his compositions. From this we may guess at the merits of those which are not extant. The Cantatas now remaining have been hitherto little examined. That of Tarquin and Lucretia was made at Rome, and its merits are much better known in Italy than in England.

We have now run through his several productions in the vocal species; and from this cursory examination I think it must appear, that even where he is least excellent on the whole, he has given such frequent, and such strong proofs of his abilities, as place him on a level with the greatest Masters, whose whole strength lay in that particular species.

In his Music for instruments there are the same marks of a great genius, and likewise some instances of great negligence. He often attended more to the effect of the whole, than to that artificial contexture of the parts, for which GEMINIANI is so justly admired.

In his Fugues and Overtures he is quite original. The Style of them is peculiar to himſelf, and no way like that of any Maſter before him. In the formation of theſe pieces, knowledge and invention ſeem to have contended for the maſtery.

Tho' no man ever introduced ſuch a number of inſtruments, yet in his Orcheſtra not one is found idle or inſignificant. On the contrary, each hath ſuch a figure and character belonging to it, as ſeems to render it not only proper and uſeful, but neceſſary and eſſential to the performance. Even thoſe which are of the loweſt order, and leaſt value, when conſidered in themſelves, from the artful and judicious manner in which they are introduced and employed, riſe into a kind of dignity and importance, of which by nature they fhould feem incapable.

Of his talents in compofing for a fingle inftrument, we need no better proofs than are given us in his Harpfichord-leffons. The firft fett, which were printed by his own order, will always be held in the higheft efteem, notwithftanding thofe real improvements in the ftyle for leffons which fome Mafters have fince hit upon. Handel's have one difadvantage, owing entirely to their peculiar excellence. The furprifing fulnefs and activity of the inner parts, increafes the difficulty of playing them to fo great a degree, that few perfons are capable of do ng them juftice. Indeed there appears to be more work in them than any one inftrument fhould feem capable of difpatching,

To

To conclude, there is in these and other parts of his works, such a fulness, force, and energy, that the harmony of HANDEL may always be compared to the antique figure of HERCULES, which seems to be nothing but muscles and sinews; as his melody may often be likened to the VENUS of MEDICIS, which is all grace and delicacy.

Whatever shall be thought of this attempt to do justice to his memory, too much reason there is for believing that the interests of religion and humanity are not so strongly guarded, or so firmly secured, as easily to spare those succours, or forego those assistances which are ministered to them from the elegant arts.

They

They refine and exalt our ideas of pleafure, which when rightly underftood, and properly purfued, is the very end of our exiftence. They improve and fettle our ideas of tafte ; which, when founded on folid and confiftent principles, explains the caufes, and heightens the effects, of whatever is beautiful or excellent, whether in the works of creation, or in the productions of human fkill.

They adorn and embellifh the face of Nature ; the talents of men they fharpen and invigorate ; the manners they civilize and polifh ; in a word, they foften the cares of life, and render its heavieft calamities much more fupportable by adding to the number of its innocent enjoyments.

The

The hopes of rendering some service to Music, and of suggesting some hints which may possibly give rise to farther enquiries into this difficult science, have induced me to subjoin to the foregoing list of Handel's works, such observations upon them, as seemed to offer themselves in the course of this review. For if the observations are just, those who are masters of the subject may be tempted to improve and extend them; and if they are erroneous, the same persons are at liberty to refute them.

At all events, such a view of the various and valuable improvements derived to Music from the incessant labours, and wonderful endowments of one * man, may serve to awaken the

* There are but a few persons, who have carefully looked over, and are thoroughly acquainted with *all* the works of Handel, and they

the attention of the Curious to those new sources of beauty and sublimity which may yet lie concealed in the regions of harmony. It may also serve to put future Artists on a more careful study of his compositions in every kind, and so check the progress of those corruptions in taste, which in every period have threatned destruction to the Art, and in none perhaps more than in the * present.

Little they only can be proper judges of his abilities. Yet a single glimpse of the Catalogue may enable us to guess at the astonishing extent of his genius: for he has not only ranged through the whole compass of his Art, but has given unquestionable proofs of his excellence in all the branches of it.

* Our most fashionable Music of late years carries hardly any appearance of knowledge or invention, hardly indeed any traces of taste or judgment. Light and trivial Airs, upheld by a thin and shadowy Harmony; an almost perpetual uniformity of style, and sameness of subject; an endless repetition of the same move-

Little indeed are the hopes of ever equalling, much lefs of excelling fo vaft a Proficient in his own way: however, as there are fo many avenues to excellence ftill open, fo many paths to glory ftill untrod, it is hoped that the example of this illuftrious Foreigner will rather prove an incentive, than a difcouragement to the induftry and genius of our own countrymen.

movements and paffages, tho' worn to rags; the barren and beggarly expedient of Pafticcios fo often practifed;—fuch a decay as this in the ftate of Mufic, (I forbear to make thofe exceptions which the Judges of the Art will make for themfelves) fhould excite fome veneration for the works of HANDEL.

F I N I S.

www.ingramcontent.com/pod-product-compliance
Lightning Source LLC
Chambersburg PA
CBHW070639050426
42451CB00008B/218